Eat Right for Less
Nutrition on a Budget

Editor . . . . *Melissa Maulding, M.S., R.D.,*
Purdue University

Project Coordinator . . . . *Deborah Garrison Lowery*

Project Advisor . . . . *Annie Watts*

Graphic Designer/
Photographer . . . . *Dan Annarino, Purdue University*

Copy Editor . . . . *Rebecca Goetz, Purdue University*

Recipe Analysis . . . . *Caroline A. Grant, M.S., R.D.*

First edition, September 2010

Eat Right for Less: Nutrition on a Budget

For information on similiar products from Purdue Extension,
visit The Education Store online

www.the-education-store.com

PURDUE EXTENSION

Printed in the United States of America

CONTENTS

Money's tight. And when you're trying to pay bills and raise a family, there isn't much time, either. Still, you want to serve healthy, great-tasting meals for your family. If this is your goal, you're in luck! As a project of the Indiana Nutrition Education Programs and Purdue University Cooperative Extension, *the recipes and tips throughout this cookbook are designed to help you cook quick, economical, healthy, and delicious meals for your family.*

How These Recipes Help

Before you plan your meals, check out all the bonus information with each recipe to see which ones best fit your needs. Here are some ways these recipes can help make your life easier:

By Saving You Time

All the recipes are designed to be fairly quick to prepare. Next to each title you'll find labels to let you know how much preparation is involved. Look for these icons to help guide you.

- ▶ Slow Cooker
- ▶ No Cook
- ▶ Quick & Easy
- ▶ Make Ahead
- ▶ Kid Friendly

Also, the recipes use common ingredients, including many staples you already have on hand, to save trips to the store.

By Fitting Your Budget

On every page, you'll find the cost of preparation for the whole recipe, as well as the cost per serving. No strange or expensive ingredients were used, and some of the recipe tips tell you how to save even more money.

By Providing Helpful Information

Tips with every recipe and throughout the cookbook chapters give you menu suggestions: how to save on cooking time or cleanup, ingredient substitution ideas, ways to save money, and more. Look for charts at the front and back of the book on topics such as buying fruits and vegetables in season, staples to keep on hand, and food safety.

By Offering Healthy Choices and Information

You'll find a complete nutritional analysis at the end of each recipe. The recipes use good-for-you ingredients such as low-fat products, whole wheat or whole grain pastas, fruits, and vegetables to help you serve healthy meals. Tips for healthy eating and cooking are also provided throughout the book.

Cooking the Healthy Way

Knowing which food options and cooking methods are better for you can help you eat healthier. Keep these tips in mind.

To Increase Fiber

▶ When you choose pastas or bread products, look for whole-grain or multi-grain varieties to include more fiber in your diet.

▶ Choose whole fruit more often than fruit juices; you'll get more fiber.

To Cut Fat and Salt

▶ Include sources of lean protein, such as fish and beans, in your diet.

▶ Use spices and herbs to season your food. They add no calories, fat, or sodium.

▶ Cook with less salt. If you need more for flavor, add it at the table.

▶ Use nonstick skillets or broiler pans. Besides making cleanup easier, they allow you to cook using less fat. A quick squirt of cooking spray on nonstick cookware will keep food from sticking and save you calories and fat.

▶ Read labels to see what's really in the food you buy. Remember that the ingredients are listed on the packages in order of the percentage contained in the product. Also look on the nutrition label for the fat, calorie, and sodium content.

▶ Include moderate amounts of salt and sugar in your diet. Too much salt can lead to high blood pressure. Sugar adds calories.

To Improve Nutrition

▶ Veggies are great. Dark green ones (like spinach) and dark orange ones (like sweet potatoes or carrots) are even better for you, thanks to the extra vitamins and nutrients they contain. Eat plenty of these.

▶ Be sure to eat calcium-rich foods such as yogurt, cottage cheese, milk, and cheese. Low-fat and fat-free versions have just as much calcium as their higher fat counterparts.

▶ Choose healthy beverages such as water, milk, and 100% juice.

▶ Know the recommended portion sizes so you don't overeat. For example, 3 ounces of meat is about the size of a deck of cards.

▶ Choose oils (olive, canola, vegetable) more often than solid fats.

▶ Add more fruits and vegetables to your diet by using them as snacks.

Eat Right for Less

- Keep your refrigerator and pantry filled with healthy staples. (See our chart on page 78.)
- Plan your meals in advance, rather than waiting until you're ready to cook. That way you'll have ingredients on hand and will be more likely to cook nutritionally balanced meals.

Cooking Economically

You don't have to spend a lot of money to serve mouth-watering meals. But, you can make your food dollars go further by following these guidelines:

By Thinking Ahead

- Shop from a list to reduce buying on impulse.
- Keep a running grocery list at home so you won't forget items on your regular shopping trip and wind up making an extra trip to the store. (You'll be likely to buy something you don't need.)
- Never shop when you're hungry!
- Clip coupons—but just for products you use. Check the supermarket sale papers before you go shopping.
- Know that products that appeal to kids often are shelved on their eye level and tend to be expensive. To head off the fuss, give your kids some healthy food options to choose before entering the store. Tell them they can pick one fruit, or help you look for a cereal that doesn't list sugar as one of the first two or three ingredients.

By Shopping Wisely

- Compare prices; store brands are almost always less expensive than national brands.
- Look for sales, especially on meat that is close to the expiration date. You can freeze it for later.
- Buy produce when it's in-season and from farmers' markets when you can.
- Buy bulk amounts of products you use often. Split the cost and food with a friend, or store the extra in your pantry or refrigerator.
- Compare prices for fresh, frozen, and canned items; most can be used interchangeably in recipes.

BREAKFAST

PUMPKIN PANCAKES WITH YOGURT-RAISIN TOPPING

Transfer leftover pumpkin from the can to a zip-top plastic freezer bag and keep it in the freezer until you make your next batch of pancakes.

Makes: 15 pancakes   Cost per Recipe: $2.80   Cost per Pancake: $0.19

2 cups low-fat vanilla yogurt, divided

½ cup raisins

1 cup all-purpose flour

1 tablespoon sugar

2 teaspoons baking powder

½ teaspoon ground cinnamon

1 cup 1% low-fat milk

2 tablespoons butter or margarine, melted

1 large egg

½ cup canned pumpkin

Nutrition Facts per Pancake with Sauce:

199 Calories; 2.5 g Total Fat (23% calories from fat); 1.5 g Saturated Fat; 16.0 g Carbohydrates; 3.6 g Protein; 21 mg Cholesterol; 0.7 g Fiber; 111 mg Sodium

1. For the topping, stir 1½ cups yogurt and raisins together in a small bowl. Cover and refrigerate.

2. Combine flour, sugar, baking powder, and cinnamon in a large bowl. Combine milk, butter, egg, pumpkin, and remaining ½ cup yogurt in a medium bowl; mix well. Add pumpkin mixture to flour mixture and stir, just until ingredients are combined. Do not overmix. The batter may be lumpy.

3. Lightly coat a griddle or skillet with cooking spray and place over medium heat. For each pancake, pour ¼ cup batter onto hot griddle. Cook 1 to 2 minutes or until bubbles appear on top. Flip pancakes and cook just until golden brown. Serve warm pancakes with 2 tablespoons topping per pancake. Sprinkle with cinnamon, if desired.

CARROT BREAKFAST BREAD

To add nuts to this or other quick bread recipes, sprinkle 2 tablespoons of chopped peanuts, pecans, or walnuts on top before baking. You can use fewer nuts this way, which means less fat and lower cost, but you still get the full flavor of the nuts.

Makes: 18 slices (½-inch each)   Cost per Recipe: $1.69   Cost per Slice: $0.09

½ cup firmly packed brown sugar

2 tablespoons vegetable oil

½ cup unsweetened applesauce

1 large egg

2 cups whole-wheat flour

2 teaspoons baking powder

½ teaspoon ground cinnamon

¼ teaspoon salt

¾ cup orange juice

1 cup finely shredded carrot

½ cup raisins or dried cranberries

Nutrition Facts per Slice:

108 Calories; 2.2 g Total Fat (18% calories from fat); 0.4 g Saturated Fat; 21.3 g Carbohydrates; 2.4 g Protein; 12 mg Cholesterol; 2.2 g Fiber; 89 mg Sodium

1. Preheat oven to 350°.

2. Combine brown sugar, oil, applesauce, and egg in a large bowl. Beat at medium speed with an electric mixer until blended.

3. Stir together flour, baking powder, cinnamon, and salt in a medium bowl. While mixing on the low speed of an electric mixer, add flour mixture to sugar mixture alternately with orange juice, beginning and ending with flour mixture. Stir in carrot and raisins.

4. Spoon batter into a 9 x 5-inch loaf pan coated with cooking spray. Bake 45 to 50 minutes or until a knife inserted in the center comes out clean. Cool in pan 10 minutes. Remove bread from pan to cool completely.

TIP Flour in the Fridge

Unlike all-purpose white flour, whole-wheat flour contains wheat germ, which can go bad quickly at room temperature. So, store it in the refrigerator or the freezer to keep the flour fresh longer.

Eat Right for Less

HAM AND CHEESE MUFFINS

Here's an easy grab-and-go breakfast for rushed mornings. Make a batch of these and store them in the freezer. Just microwave one for a few seconds to reheat. Add a banana or apple slices and milk for a complete meal.

Makes: 12 muffins   Cost per Recipe: $3.24   Cost per Muffin: $0.27

1 cup all-purpose flour

1 cup whole-wheat flour

1 tablespoon baking powder

½ teaspoon salt

1 cup low-fat buttermilk

3 tablespoons vegetable oil

1 large egg

1¼ cups (8 ounces) chopped, cooked lean ham

1½ cups (6 ounces) shredded 50% reduced-fat Cheddar cheese

Nutrition Facts per Muffin:

217 Calories; 8.3 g Total Fat (34% calories from fat); 2.7 g Saturated Fat; 24.9 g Carbohydrates; 11.6 g Protein; 34 mg Cholesterol; 1.8 g Fiber; 531 mg Sodium

1. Preheat oven to 400°.

2. Combine all-purpose and whole-wheat flours, baking powder, and salt in a large bowl. Combine buttermilk, oil, and egg in a medium bowl; mix well. Stir in ham and cheese.

3. Add ham mixture to flour mixture, stirring with a rubber spatula, just until mixture is combined. Do not overmix.

4. Coat cups of a muffin pan with cooking spray. Spoon batter into cups, filling ¾ full. Bake 20 minutes or until browned. Remove muffins from pan and cool.

TIP Substitute for Buttermilk
No buttermilk on hand? Just add 1 tablespoon of lemon juice or vinegar to a measuring cup, then add regular milk to equal 1 cup. Let the mixture stand 10 minutes, and it's ready to use as a buttermilk substitute.

RISE AND SHINE PEACH SCONES

An easy way to chop canned peaches and avoid extra cleanup is to chop them right in the can with kitchen scissors. (This works for canned tomatoes, too.) Save the peach juice you drain off to add to smoothies, or let the kids drink it.

Makes: 20 scones   Cost per Recipe: $2.39   Cost per Scone: $0.12

3 cups plus 3 tablespoons all-purpose flour

¾ cup sugar

1 tablespoon plus 2 teaspoons baking powder

½ teaspoon baking soda

6 tablespoons cold butter or margarine, cut into pieces

½ cup low-fat buttermilk

1 large egg

½ teaspoon vanilla extract

1 (15-ounce) can sliced peaches in light syrup, drained and chopped (about 1 cup)

⅓ cup sugar

2 tablespoons low-fat buttermilk

Nutrition Facts per Scone:

161 Calories; 4.2 g Total Fat (23% calories from fat); 2.3 g Saturated Fat; 28.1 g Carbohydrates; 2.7 g Protein; 20 mg Cholesterol; 0.6 g Fiber; 191 mg Sodium

1. Preheat oven to 375°. Combine flour, ¾ cup sugar, baking powder, and baking soda in a large bowl. Add butter, and using two knives or a pastry blender, cut in butter until crumbly.

2. Combine ½ cup buttermilk, egg, vanilla, and peaches in a medium bowl. Stir peach mixture into flour mixture, stirring with a fork until ingredients are combined and begin to pull away from the bowl. (Dough will be sticky.)

3. Using floured hands, shape dough into rounds (like biscuits) using ¼ cup dough for each scone.

4. Place on a baking sheet coated with cooking spray. Or, spoon mixture into cups of a muffin pan coated with cooking spray, filling cups ½ full.

5. Combine ⅓ cup sugar and 2 tablespoons buttermilk in a small bowl. Brush mixture on top of unbaked dough. (Try not to get sugar mixture on baking sheet or muffin pan or it will burn onto the pan during baking.) Bake 15 to 20 minutes or until golden brown on top.

Eat Right for Less

BERRY FRENCH TOAST

If you have leftover French toast, store it in the refrigerator in a zip-top plastic bag. Reheat it the next day by popping the slices in the toaster for a super-quick breakfast. Pick fresh blueberries at local pick-your-own farms or farmers' markets in summer when the berries are in season, then freeze them, and you'll save even more money on this recipe.

Makes: 8 slices French toast   Cost per Recipe: $4.58   Cost per Slice: $0. 57

4 large eggs

⅓ cup 1% low-fat milk

1 teaspoon vanilla extract

Pinch ground cinnamon

8 slices whole-wheat bread

Powdered sugar

2 cups fresh or canned blueberries and/or raspberries

Maple syrup (optional)

Nutrition Facts per Slice:

145 Calories; 4.4 g Total Fat (27% calories from fat); 1.1 g Saturated Fat; 21 g Carbohydrates; 6.5 g Protein; 166 mg Cholesterol; 2.8 g Fiber; 187 mg Sodium

1. Beat eggs in a large bowl with a whisk or a fork. Stir in milk, vanilla, and cinnamon.

2. Dip bread in egg mixture, 1 slice at a time, and soak 1 minute, turning once.

3. Coat a large, nonstick skillet with cooking spray and place over medium heat. Add egg-soaked bread slices to hot skillet, and cook about 4 minutes on each side, or until golden brown.

4. To serve, sprinkle French toast with powdered sugar and top with berries. Serve with warm maple syrup, if desired.

COMPANY SAUSAGE STRATA

This hearty recipe bakes for 45 minutes, but you can make it the day before, then cover and refrigerate it before baking. Bake it the next day and add fresh fruit and milk for a complete meal.

Makes: 9 servings   Cost per Recipe: $6.25   Cost per Serving: $0. 70

4 slices whole-wheat bread, torn (2 cups)

½ teaspoon olive oil

½ cup chopped onion

½ cup chopped red bell pepper

7 ounces reduced-fat smoked turkey sausage, thinly sliced

1 cup shredded part-skim mozzarella cheese

¼ cup grated Parmesan cheese

3 large eggs

2 large egg whites

1½ cups fat-free milk

½ teaspoon hot sauce

½ teaspoon salt

½ teaspoon pepper

Nutrition Facts per Serving:

147 Calories; 5.7 g Total Fat (35% calories from fat); 2.7 g Saturated Fat; 12.7 g Carbohydrates; 11.4 g Protein; 61 mg Cholesterol; 1.3 g Fiber; 528 mg Sodium

1. Preheat oven to 350°.

2. Arrange bread pieces in bottom of a 9-inch-square baking dish coated with cooking spray.

3. Add olive oil to a nonstick skillet and place over medium-high heat. Add onion and bell pepper; cook 4 minutes, stirring frequently. Add sausage to skillet and cook, stirring often, until vegetables are tender and sausage is lightly browned, about 3 minutes. Remove from heat and spread evenly over bread in baking dish. Top evenly with mozzarella and Parmesan cheeses.

4. Beat eggs and egg whites in a medium bowl with a whisk or a fork; stir in milk and seasonings. Pour over cheese. (At this point, the strata may be covered and refrigerated overnight.) Bake 45 minutes or until set in the center. Remove from oven and let stand 10 minutes before serving.

TIP Kids Can Cook, Too

Get children involved with cooking by letting them do easy tasks like tearing bread for this recipe. Other simple cooking jobs for little ones include washing fruit and vegetables, stirring batter, filling muffin pans, or adding spices to mixtures.

Eat Right for Less

TEX-MEX BREAKFAST QUESADILLAS

For breakfast-in-the-car, wrap these quesadillas in waxed paper to eat like sandwiches.

Makes: 6 servings   Cost per Recipe: $4.84   Cost per Serving: $0. 81

1 cup (4 ounces) shredded 50% reduced-fat pepper jack cheese

6 (8-inch) 96% fat-free whole-wheat flour tortillas

¼ cup sliced green onions

4 large eggs

4 large egg whites

¼ cup plus 2 tablespoons salsa

Nutrition Facts per Serving:

252 Calories; 9.6 g Total Fat (34% calories from fat); 3.4 g Saturated Fat; 27.4 g Carbohydrates; 15.6 g Protein; 155 mg Cholesterol; 3.4 g Fiber; 344 mg Sodium

1. Sprinkle cheese evenly on half of each tortilla. Top each with 1 tablespoon green onions.

2. Coat a large nonstick skillet with cooking spray and place over medium heat until hot. Beat eggs and egg whites in a medium bowl, with a whisk or a fork. Pour egg mixture into skillet. As eggs begin to set, gently pull the eggs across the skillet with an inverted turner, forming large, soft curds. Continue to cook, pulling, lifting, and folding eggs, until set and no visible egg liquid remains. Do not stir constantly.

3. Spoon eggs evenly over the cheese on each tortilla. Fold tortilla over filling to cover, pressing gently. Clean skillet; coat with cooking spray, and place over medium-low heat until hot. Toast quesadillas, one at a time, 1 to 2 minutes per side, just until cheese melts. Cut into wedges, and serve with salsa. Serve with low-fat sour cream, if desired.

VEGGIE-CHEESE FRITTATA

Potatoes give a nice, crunchy crust to this skillet-cooked egg recipe. Substitute your family's favorite vegetables such as chopped broccoli, carrots, tomatoes, peas, or whatever's in your fridge. Cheddar cheese is a good substitute for feta. When fresh herbs are in season—especially basil, oregano, thyme, or parsley—add those instead of the Italian seasoning.

Makes: 4 servings   Cost per Recipe: $3.11   Cost per Serving: $0. 78

2 cups peeled, shredded potato

½ cup chopped onion

½ cup chopped zucchini

⅓ cup chopped red bell pepper

2 large eggs

2 large egg whites

1½ teaspoons Italian seasoning

½ teaspoon salt

½ teaspoon pepper

¼ cup reduced-fat feta cheese

Nutrition Facts per Serving:

182 Calories; 4.0 g Total Fat (20% calories from fat); 1.6 g Saturated Fat; 27.2 g Carbohydrates; 9.3 g Protein; 110 mg Cholesterol; 3.1 g Fiber; 442 mg Sodium

1. Preheat oven to 450°.

2. Coat an ovenproof nonstick skillet with cooking spray and place over medium-high heat until hot.

3. Add potato, onion, zucchini, and red bell pepper. Cook, stirring often until potatoes are lightly browned, 7 to 8 minutes.

4. Beat eggs, egg whites, and seasonings in a medium bowl using a whisk or a fork. Pour over vegetables in skillet. Reduce heat to medium-low, and cook 2 to 3 minutes without stirring, just until egg mixture is set. Sprinkle evenly with cheese.

5. Place skillet in oven and bake 3 to 4 minutes or until cheese is lightly browned. Cut into wedges to serve.

TIP Best Way to Beat Eggs

Although it's fine to use a fork to beat eggs, a whisk is a handy tool that helps beat the eggs quickly and easily, and it helps blend the yolks and whites thoroughly. You can get one for just a couple of dollars anywhere kitchen utensils are sold. A hand or electric mixer works well, too.

Eat Right for Less

BANANA BREAD OATMEAL

To toast pecans for this recipe, spread them on a plate and microwave on HIGH for 1 minute, stir, and microwave 30 seconds at a time until toasted. Or, bake them at 350° for about 5 minutes or until golden brown.

Makes: 6 servings   Cost per Recipe: $2.43   Cost per Serving: $0. 41

3 cups fat-free milk

3 tablespoons firmly packed light brown sugar

¾ teaspoon ground cinnamon

¼ teaspoon ground nutmeg

¼ teaspoon salt

2 cups quick or old-fashioned oats, uncooked

1 cup mashed bananas (about 2 medium)

2 tablespoons coarsely chopped toasted pecans

Nutrition Facts per Serving:

234 Calories; 3.9 g Total Fat (15% calories from fat); 0.6 g Saturated Fat; 42.1 g Carbohydrates; 8.6 g Protein; 3 mg Cholesterol; 4.5 g Fiber; 153 mg Sodium

1. Combine milk, brown sugar, cinnamon, nutmeg, and salt in a medium saucepan. Place over medium-high heat and bring to a gentle boil (watch carefully). Stir in oats; return to a boil; and reduce heat to medium. Cook 1 minute for quick oats or 5 minutes for old-fashioned oats, or until most of the liquid is absorbed, stirring occasionally.

2. Remove from heat and stir in bananas and pecans. Spoon into individual bowls and top with yogurt, sliced bananas, and pecan halves, if desired.

PINEAPPLE-BANANA SMOOTHIE

No time to eat? This fruity smoothie makes a yummy, healthy breakfast-to-go. Adding the ice makes it extra slushy.

Makes: 3 servings   Cost per Recipe: $1.79   Cost per Serving: $0. 60

2 medium bananas, peeled and frozen

1 cup non-fat vanilla yogurt

½ cup orange juice

1 (8-ounce) can crushed pineapple, or pineapple tidbits or chunks in juice, undrained

10 cubes ice (optional)

1. Combine all ingredients in container of an electric blender. Process until smooth.

2. Pour into glasses and serve.

Nutrition Facts per Serving:

212 Calories; 0.2 g Total Fat (1% calories from fat); 0.1 g Saturated Fat; 50 g Carbohydrates; 5.5 g Protein; 1 mg Cholesterol; 3.4 g Fiber; 57 mg Sodium

 Mushy Bananas?
Don't throw away bananas when they get too soft to eat. Instead, peel and store them in the freezer. The frozen bananas will be ready to use to make smoothies or banana bread, or to mash into oatmeal.

Eat Right for Less

MAIN DISHES

* If no external source is listed in parentheses for a recipe,
  the recipe was developed by the authors.

APRICOT CHICKEN-VEGETABLE STIR-FRY

You can use any combination of vegetables in this recipe. A 12-ounce package containing fresh broccoli, cauliflower, and carrots from the produce section is the perfect amount to use. If you buy the produce separately and cut your own slices and flowerets, just make sure the total amount of vegetables equals 4 cups. Sugar snap peas would also be a good vegetable to include in this stir-fry. They're sweet and crispy.

Makes: 4 servings   Cost per Recipe: $8.84   Cost per Serving: $2.21

½ cup apricot preserves

2 tablespoons fat-free chicken broth

1 tablespoon reduced-sodium soy sauce

½ teaspoon garlic powder

½ teaspoon ground ginger

½ teaspoon olive oil

4 (4-ounce) boneless, skinless chicken breast halves, cut in ½-inch strips

1 (12-ounce) package fresh broccoli, cauliflower, and carrots (4 cups)

2 cups hot cooked regular or brown rice (cooked without salt or fat)

1. Combine apricot preserves, broth, soy sauce, garlic powder, and ginger in a small bowl.

2. Add olive oil to a nonstick skillet and place over medium-high heat. Add chicken to skillet and cook for 3 minutes, stirring constantly until lightly browned. Add half of apricot mixture to skillet, and continue cooking 1 minute or until chicken is done. Transfer chicken to serving bowl.

3. Add vegetables and remaining apricot mixture to skillet and cook 4 minutes, stirring constantly until vegetables are crisp-tender. Add vegetables to chicken. Serve over rice.

Nutrition Facts per Serving:

358 Calories; 3.8 g Total Fat (10% from fat); 0.9 g Saturated Fat; 54.1 g Carbohydrates;
27.7 g Protein; 63 mg Cholesterol; 3.3 g Fiber; 118 mg Sodium

Eat Right for Less

CHEESY CHICKEN CRUNCHES

This recipe for chicken fingers is a great one to use to introduce your children to cooking. Put the cornflakes in a zip-top plastic bag, seal it, and let the kids crush the cereal into crumbs. They can help dip the chicken in the flour, egg, and cheese mixtures, too. If the kids like dipping sauces, serve the chicken fingers with honey or fat-free ranch dressing.

Makes: 6 servings   Cost per Recipe: $10.35   Cost per Serving: $1.73

1 cup all-purpose flour

¼ teaspoon salt

¼ teaspoon pepper

4 large egg whites

½ cup fat-free milk

1½ cups crushed cornflakes cereal

1 cup (4 ounces) shredded, 50% reduced-fat cheddar cheese

6 (4-ounce) boneless, skinless chicken breast halves, cut into 1 x 4-inch strips

Nutrition Facts per Serving:

282 Calories; 5.7 g Total Fat (18% from fat); 2.6 g Saturated Fat; 22.6 g Carbohydrates; 33.3 g Protein; 72 mg Cholesterol; 0.9 g Fiber; 359 mg Sodium

1. Preheat oven to 375°. Coat a large baking sheet with cooking spray.

2. Combine flour, salt, and pepper in a shallow bowl.

3. Beat egg whites and milk in a second shallow bowl.

4. Combine cornflakes and cheese in a third shallow bowl.

5. Dip each chicken strip first in flour mixture, then in egg mixture, then in cheese mixture. Arrange strips on prepared baking sheet. Bake 12 minutes, turn chicken strips, and bake 8 to 12 additional minutes.

Note: Coated, unbaked chicken strips may be frozen on a baking sheet. When frozen, transfer strips to a large zip-top plastic freezer bag, seal, and store. Chicken may be baked without thawing. To bake, place frozen chicken strips on a baking sheet coated with cooking spray and bake at 375° for 25 minutes.

EASY MOZZARELLA CHICKEN BAKE

This recipe is handy to keep in the freezer. Place it in the refrigerator to thaw in the morning and it will be ready to bake for supper. Just add a salad and bread and the meal is complete. It's also a good recipe to have on hand when you need to take a meal to a friend.

Makes: 8 servings   Cost per recipe: $14.41   Cost per serving: $1.80

1 cup reduced-fat Italian dressing

8 (4-ounce) boneless, skinless chicken breast halves

½ teaspoon olive oil

1 (26-ounce) can or jar garlic-and-herb or regular spaghetti sauce

2 cups (8 ounces) shredded, part-skim mozzarella cheese

4 cups hot, cooked regular or brown rice (cooked without salt or fat) or hot, cooked spaghetti

Nutrition Facts per Serving:

387 Calories; 11.7 g Total Fat (27% from fat); 4.6 g Saturated Fat; 32.7 g Carbohydrates; 36.7 g Protein; 83 mg Cholesterol; 1.5 g Fiber; 694 mg Sodium

TIP Save on Chicken

When boneless, skinless chicken is on sale, buy extra and freeze it. Simply trim the chicken and place it on a baking pan in a single layer. Place the tray in the freezer. When the chicken is frozen, remove it from the tray and store it in zip-top plastic freezer bags.

1. Place Italian dressing in a large zip-top plastic bag. Add chicken, seal top, and refrigerate at least 30 minutes. (May be refrigerated overnight.)

2. Preheat oven to 350°. Coat a 13 x 9-inch baking dish with cooking spray.

3. Remove chicken from zip-top bag and discard dressing. Add olive oil to nonstick skillet and place over medium-high heat. Add chicken to hot skillet and cook 1 minute on each side, or just until browned. Remove chicken from skillet.

4. Pour just enough spaghetti sauce in prepared baking dish to cover bottom. Arrange browned chicken over sauce. Top chicken with remaining sauce. Sprinkle mozzarella cheese evenly over chicken.

5. Bake, uncovered, 25 minutes or until bubbly. Serve over rice.

Note: This dish may be covered with foil and frozen before baking. To bake, allow casserole to thaw overnight in refrigerator, then bake as instructed above.

Eat Right for Less

ROSEMARY LEMON CHICKEN BREASTS

When you cook chicken with skin, tucking flavorful ingredients such as herbs, garlic, lemon slices, or onion underneath the skin is an easy way to add extra flavor. The skin helps keep the meat juicy and moist while it cooks.

Makes: 5 servings   Cost per Recipe: $8.46   Cost per Serving: $1.69

5 bone-in chicken breast halves with skin (about 6 ounces each)

¼ teaspoon salt

½ teaspoon garlic powder

10 thin lemon slices

5 (3-inch) sprigs fresh rosemary or 2 teaspoons dried, crushed rosemary

½ teaspoon black pepper

Nutrition Facts per Serving:

205 Calories; 6.7 g Total Fat (29% from fat); 1.8 g Saturated Fat;
0.7 g Carbohydrates; 34.6 g Protein;
93 mg Cholesterol; 0.2 g Fiber;
199 mg Sodium

1. Preheat oven to 350°. Coat a 13 x 9-inch baking dish with cooking spray.

2. Using your fingers, pull skin away from chicken without removing skin. Rub salt and garlic powder on chicken breasts under the skin. For each breast half, tuck two lemon slices between skin and chicken; add a sprig of rosemary on top of lemon slices. Pull skin over lemon and rosemary to cover as much of chicken as possible.

3. Place chicken breasts in prepared baking dish. Spray tops of chicken breasts with butter-flavored cooking spray. Sprinkle evenly with pepper. Bake, uncovered, 40 minutes or until thickest parts of chicken breasts are done.

HERBED TURKEY BURGERS

The oregano-mayonnaise is especially delicious served in other recipes, too. Try it with fresh tomato slices or fish, or on chicken or deli sandwiches. "Sandwich rounds" take the place of traditional buns. Look for these very thin sandwich breads and you'll save about half the calories and fat of traditional whole-wheat sandwich buns. What they're called varies by brand—you'll find them labeled sandwich rounds, sandwich thins, deli flats, or thin buns.

Makes: 8 servings   Cost per Recipe: $9.28   Cost per Serving: $1.16

½ cup light mayonnaise

3 tablespoons chopped fresh oregano or 2¼ teaspoons dried oregano, divided

2 pounds lean ground turkey

¼ cup finely chopped onion

¼ cup barbecue sauce

8 multi-grain thin sandwich rounds, split

8 slices fresh tomato

Nutrition Facts per Serving:

306 Calories; 11.7 g Total Fat (34% from fat); 2.5 g Saturated Fat; 26.2 g Carbohydrates; 27.3 g Protein; 66 mg Cholesterol; 5.3 g Fiber; 495 mg Sodium

1. Combine mayonnaise and 1 tablespoon fresh or ¾ teaspoon dried oregano in a small bowl. Cover and refrigerate.

2. Combine turkey, onion, remaining 2 tablespoons fresh or 1½ teaspoons dried oregano, and barbecue sauce in a large bowl. Form mixture into 8 equal patties (mixture will be soft).

3. Coat a large nonstick skillet with cooking spray and place over medium-high heat. Place turkey patties in hot skillet, and cook 5 to 7 minutes on each side, or until done.

4. Spread each sandwich round half with 1½ teaspoons oregano-mayonnaise. Place turkey burgers on bottom half of each round, top each with a tomato slice and top half of sandwich round.

TIP Herbs for Flavor

Herbs are a good way to add flavor without adding salt or fat. You can substitute dried herbs for fresh, but remember to use less of the dried version. For each tablespoon of fresh chopped herbs, use 1 teaspoon of dried or ¼ teaspoon of ground herbs.

Eat Right for Less

PORCUPINE MEATBALLS

Kids will love the way the rice pops out, making each meatball look like a porcupine. Serve these big meatballs with steamed broccoli or carrots, fresh fruit, and bread to round out the meal.

Makes: 4 servings   Cost per Recipe: $4.52   Cost per Serving: $1.13

1 pound 96% lean ground beef

¼ cup finely chopped onion

¼ cup uncooked regular or brown rice

1 large egg white

1 tablespoon Worcestershire sauce

1 teaspoon pepper

¼ teaspoon salt

½ teaspoon vegetable oil

1 (15-ounce) can tomato sauce

1 teaspoon Italian seasoning

2 tablespoons grated Parmesan cheese

Nutrition Facts per Serving:

229 Calories; 5.6 g Total Fat (22% from fat); 2.3 g Saturated Fat; 19.6 g Carbohydrates; 25.4 g Protein; 54 mg Cholesterol; 2.3 g Fiber; 876 mg Sodium

1. Combine beef, onion, rice, egg white, Worcestershire sauce, pepper, and salt in a bowl. Mix well and form into 8 equal-size balls. Place oil in a nonstick skillet over medium-high heat. Add meatballs, and brown on all sides. Remove meatballs from skillet, and wipe skillet with a paper towel to remove fat.

2. Add tomato sauce and Italian seasoning to skillet. Return meatballs to skillet, turning to coat meatballs with sauce. Cover, reduce heat to low, and simmer 20 minutes or until meatballs are done.

3. Transfer meatballs to a serving plate, and pour sauce over top. Sprinkle with Parmesan cheese.

CHEESE-STUFFED MEATLOAF

Ground beef labels may list ground sirloin, ground chuck, ground round, or just ground beef. But for the lowest in fat, pay attention to the lean-to-fat percent on the label. Ground beef considered lean is at least 90% or more lean.

Makes: 6 servings   Cost per Recipe: $7.77   Cost per Serving: $1.30

½ teaspoon olive oil

½ teaspoon minced garlic

¾ cup chopped onion

¾ cup chopped green bell pepper

1½ pounds 96% lean ground beef

2 egg whites

1 cup torn bread crumbs or quick-cooking oats

¼ teaspoon salt

1 cup ketchup, divided

¾ cup (3 ounces) shredded 50% reduced-fat cheddar cheese

2 tablespoons apple jelly

Nutrition Facts per Serving:

275 Calories; 7.7 g Total Fat (25% from fat); 3.7 g Saturated Fat; 21.2 g Carbohydrates; 31.1 g Protein; 68 mg Cholesterol; 0.9 g Fiber; 784 mg Sodium

1. Preheat oven to 350°. Coat a 10-inch deep-dish pie plate or a 2-quart baking dish with cooking spray.

2. Place olive oil in a nonstick skillet over medium-high heat. Add garlic, onion, and bell pepper to skillet; cook, stirring often, 5 minutes or until onion is tender. Transfer vegetables to a large bowl.

3. Add ground beef, egg whites, bread, salt, and ½ cup ketchup to bowl with vegetables; mix well. Pat half of mixture into prepared dish. Sprinkle with cheese. Top with remaining beef mixture and press together to seal meat over cheese.

4. Combine remaining ½ cup ketchup and apple jelly. Spread evenly on top of beef mixture. Bake 40 minutes or until done.

TIP How to Freeze Ground Beef

It's fine to freeze ground beef in the original packaging from the grocery store for up to two weeks. If you plan to store it longer, remove it from the original package and wrap it in freezer paper, aluminum foil, or a zip-top freezer bag to prevent freezer burn.

Eat Right for Less

CAJUN BEEF & BEAN STEW

Disposable slow cooker liners are great to save on cleanup if you make this recipe in the slow cooker. If you don't use a liner, then just coat the inside of the slow cooker stoneware with cooking spray to make cleaning easier.

Makes: 8 servings   Cost per Recipe: $13.22   Cost per Serving: $1.65

2 pounds beef stew meat, cut in 1-inch pieces

1 (10¾-ounce) can condensed tomato soup

½ cup 99% fat-free beef broth or water

1 (14½-ounce) can stewed tomatoes

4 large carrots, cut in 1-inch pieces

2 teaspoons Cajun seasoning

2 (15-ounce) cans dark red kidney beans, undrained

4 cups cooked rice (cooked without salt or fat)

1. Brown beef over medium-high heat in a large Dutch oven or heavy kettle; drain off fat. Add remaining ingredients, except rice, to Dutch oven. Bring to a boil; reduce heat, and simmer, covered, 2½ hours until beef is tender, stirring occasionally to prevent sticking.

2. Spoon ½ cup rice into each of eight large soup bowls. Spoon the stew over rice.

Slow Cooker Directions:
Combine all ingredients, except rice, in a slow cooker. Cover and cook on LOW 8 to 9 hours or on HIGH 4 to 5 hours or until beef is done.

Nutrition Facts per Serving:

424 Calories; 8.9 g Total Fat (19% calories from fat); 3.1 g Saturated Fat; 53.4 g Carbohydrates; 31.9 g Protein; 71 mg Cholesterol; 10.6 g Fiber; 816 mg Sodium

JUICY POT ROAST WITH VEGETABLES

The slow cooker is an excellent way to cook less tender (and less expensive) meats like rump roast. The long, slow cooking makes it tender enough to pull apart with a fork. It's also convenient to put dinner on in the morning and have it done when you get home for supper.

Makes: 12 servings   Cost per Recipe: $7.74   Cost per Serving: $0.65

1 (3-pound) boneless beef rump roast

¼ teaspoon garlic powder

1 (10¾-ounce) can condensed tomato soup

½ cup water

¼ cup cider vinegar

2 tablespoons Worcestershire sauce

½ teaspoon ground oregano

½ teaspoon celery seeds

½ teaspoon pepper

¼ teaspoon salt

4 large carrots, cut in 2-inch pieces

4 medium potatoes, scrubbed and quartered

Nutrition Facts per Serving:

371 Calories; 10.1 g Fat (25% calories from fat); 3.6 g Saturated Fat; 17.7 g Carbohydrates; 49.5 g Protein; 107 mg Cholesterol; 1.8 g Fiber; 319 mg Sodium

1. Cut away excess fat from roast. Sprinkle roast with garlic powder.

2. Place a large Dutch oven or heavy kettle over high heat until hot. Add roast, turning to brown on all sides.

3. Combine soup, water, vinegar, Worcestershire sauce, oregano, celery seeds, pepper, and salt; pour over the roast. Bring liquid to a boil; cover, reduce heat, and simmer 1½ hours. Add carrots and potatoes; cover and simmer 1 hour or until roast and vegetables are tender.

Slow Cooker Directions:
After trimming and browning roast as instructed above, place roast, fat side up, in a slow cooker. Combine remaining ingredients and add to slow cooker. Cover, and cook on LOW 8 to 9 hours or on HIGH 4 to 5 hours, or until roast is tender enough to pull apart with a fork.

TIP Don't Peek in the Slow Cooker!
Try to resist the temptation to lift the lid of a slow cooker during cooking. If you do remove the lid and let out the heat, add 20 to 30 minutes extra cooking time.

Eat Right for Less

HAM-TOPPED SWEET POTATOES

Prepare the ham mixture and bake the sweet potatoes in advance to turn this into a make-ahead recipe. Reheat both in the microwave when you're ready to serve dinner. This recipe is a great way to use leftover ham.

Makes: 4 servings   Cost per Recipe: $8.46   Cost per Serving: $2.12

4 medium sweet potatoes

1 (15¼-ounce) can pineapple tidbits, undrained

1 tablespoon vinegar

2 teaspoons cornstarch

1 teaspoon dry mustard

1 tablespoon brown sugar

¼ cup dried cranberries or raisins

2½ cups chopped cooked lean ham

Nutrition Facts per Serving:

372 Calories; 5.0 g Total Fat (12% from fat); 1.5 g Saturated Fat; 61 g Carbohydrates; 21 g Protein; 45 mg Cholesterol; 5.4 g Fiber; 1,062 mg Sodium

TIP Reduce the Sodium
Ham can be high in sodium, so if you're watching sodium in your diet, substitute lean, chopped turkey for ham in this recipe or others. Just cook a turkey tenderloin in a skillet with ½ teaspoon olive oil, then chop the meat. The sodium will be reduced to 112 mg per serving.

1. Preheat oven to 350°. Wash sweet potatoes and wrap each in foil. Bake 45 minutes or until done. OR, to microwave sweet potatoes, pierce each in several places with a fork. (Do not wrap in foil.) Arrange end to end in a circle. Microwave on HIGH 25 minutes or until done. Keep warm.

2. Drain pineapple tidbits, reserving juice. Add enough water to juice to equal ½ cup. Add vinegar, cornstarch, mustard, and brown sugar to pineapple juice, stirring well.

3. Add pineapple juice mixture in a large skillet over medium-high heat. Stir in cranberries. Bring mixture to a boil, and boil 1 minute or until thickened, stirring constantly. Stir in ham and pineapple tidbits. Cook, stirring occasionally, 3 minutes or until thoroughly heated.

4. Split sweet potatoes lengthwise and mash slightly. Spoon ham mixture evenly over split potatoes. Serve hot.

LEMON PEPPER PORK CHOPS

The thinner the cut of meat, the quicker it cooks. These thin-sliced pork chops can be on the table in less than 10 minutes.

Makes: 3 servings   Cost per Recipe: $5.56   Cost per Serving: $1.85

6 thin-sliced, boneless pork loin chops (about 12 ounces)

1 teaspoon pepper

4 teaspoons lemon juice

½ teaspoon vegetable oil

¼ cup fat-free chicken broth

2 tablespoons cider vinegar

1 tablespoon butter or margarine

Nutrition Facts per Serving:

204 Calories; 11.1 g Total Fat (49% from fat); 4.9 g Saturated Fat; 1.0 g Carbohydrates; 23.5 g Protein; 77 mg Cholesterol; 0.2 g Fiber; 119 mg Sodium

1. Sprinkle chops on both sides with pepper and drizzle with lemon juice.

2. Heat oil in a large, nonstick skillet over medium-high heat. Add chops and cook 3 minutes on each side or until done. Transfer chops to a serving platter and keep warm.

3. Add broth and vinegar to skillet and cook, stirring often, 1 to 2 minutes or until liquid begins to appear thick, like syrup. Add butter and stir until blended. Pour over chops.

MARINATED PINEAPPLE PORK CHOPS

The longer you marinate the pork chops, the more flavorful they will be. You can save cooking time, too, by putting the chops in to marinate the night before you plan to cook them. Then, cooking time is only 10 minutes.

Makes: 8 servings   Cost per Recipe: $14.01   Cost per Serving: $1.75

8 thin-sliced pork loin chops (about 2¼ pounds)

1 (20-ounce) can pineapple slices, undrained

1 cup fat-free Catalina or French salad dressing

¼ cup reduced-sodium soy sauce

2 tablespoons lemon juice

½ teaspoon garlic powder

¼ teaspoon ground ginger

8 maraschino cherries, optional

Nutrition Facts per Serving:

191 Calories; 5.9 g Total Fat (27% calories from fat); 2.1 g Saturated Fat; 11.7 g Carbohydrates; 21.7 g Protein; 58 mg Cholesterol; 1.1 g Fiber; 306 mg Sodium

1. Trim off bones from pork chops, and discard bones. Drain juice from pineapple. Measure ¼ cup pineapple juice and place in a large zip-top plastic bag. Add dressing, soy sauce, lemon juice, garlic powder, and ground ginger to pineapple juice in zip-top bag. Seal bag and mash with hands to mix well.

2. Measure ¼ cup marinade into a separate container and set aside for basting during cooking. Add pork to large zip-top plastic bag, seal top, and refrigerate 1 to 12 hours.

3. Preheat broiler. Line bottom of a broiler pan with aluminum foil. Coat top of broiler rack with cooking spray. Remove pork chops from marinade, and discard marinade. Arrange chops on broiler rack. Place a pineapple ring on top of each chop. Brush with reserved ¼ cup marinade. Broil chops 5½ inches from heat, 8 to 10 minutes or until chops are done.

4. Arrange chops on a serving platter. Top each with a maraschino cherry in center of each pineapple ring, if desired.

CRUSTLESS SPINACH QUICHE

This recipe fits in the menu any time of the day—breakfast, brunch, lunch, or dinner. For breakfast or brunch, serve it with a fruit salad and a muffin. For lunch or supper, pair it with fresh, sliced tomatoes and cucumbers, and whole-wheat rolls.

Makes: 4 servings   Cost per Recipe: $5.66   Cost per Serving: $1.42

1 teaspoon canola or vegetable oil

1 cup chopped onion (1 medium)

1 (10-ounce) package frozen, chopped spinach, thawed and drained

1½ cups (6 ounces) shredded, 75% reduced-fat cheddar cheese

6 large egg whites

1 large egg

⅓ cup fat-free cottage cheese

¼ teaspoon ground red pepper

⅛ teaspoon salt

⅛ teaspoon ground nutmeg

Nutrition Facts per Serving:

198 Calories; 6.9 g Total Fat (31% from fat); 2.9 g Saturated Fat; 8.3 g Carbohydrates; 26.5 g Protein; 69 mg Cholesterol; 2.0 g Fiber; 547 mg Sodium

1. Preheat oven to 375°. Coat a 9-inch pie plate with cooking spray.

2. Heat oil in a nonstick skillet over medium-high heat. Add onion; cook, stirring often, 5 minutes or until onion is soft. Add spinach and stir until moisture evaporates, about 3 additional minutes.

3. Sprinkle cheese evenly in the bottom of prepared pie plate. Top with spinach mixture.

4. Beat egg whites, egg, cottage cheese, and spices in a medium bowl using a whisk. Pour mixture over spinach.

5. Bake 30 minutes or until set. Let stand 5 minutes before cutting into wedges to serve.

TIP How to Store Yolks and Whites

To store leftover egg yolks, place them in a container and cover them with water. Cover tightly, and they will keep in the refrigerator for up to 3 days. If you have leftover egg whites, place one each in sections of an ice cube tray and freeze. Pop out the egg white cubes when frozen and store them in the freezer in a zip-top plastic freezer bag.

Eat Right for Less

VEGETABLE LASAGNA

Get a step ahead of dinner by making this recipe the day before. Just refrigerate it unbaked, then it's ready for the oven when you are. It's an entire meal in itself, so just add some crusty French bread and dinner is done!

Makes: 8 servings   Cost per Recipe: $8.15   Cost per Serving: $1.02

9 uncooked lasagna noodles

½ teaspoon olive oil

1 cup sliced fresh mushrooms

4 cups thinly sliced zucchini (about 3 medium)

1 cup shredded carrot

2½ cups prepared garlic-and-herb or regular spaghetti sauce

1 teaspoon dried basil

1½ cups 1% low-fat cottage cheese

½ cup low-fat sour cream

1½ cups (6 ounces) shredded, part-skim mozzarella cheese

Nutrition Facts per Serving:

320 Calories; 8.5 g Total Fat (24% from fat); 4.1 g Saturated Fat; 44.8 g Carbohydrates; 19.0 g Protein; 20 mg Cholesterol; 3.2 g Fiber; 605 mg Sodium

1. Preheat oven to 350°. Coat a 13 x 9-inch baking dish with cooking spray.

2. Cook lasagna noodles according to package directions. Drain and set aside.

3. Place olive oil in a large, nonstick skillet and place over medium-high heat. Add mushrooms and zucchini, and cook, stirring often, 5 to 7 minutes, or until crisp-tender.

4. Add carrot, spaghetti sauce, and basil to skillet. Cook, stirring often, 1 additional minute.

5. Combine cottage cheese and sour cream in a small bowl.

6. To assemble lasagna, spread one-third of vegetable-sauce mixture in bottom of prepared baking dish. Arrange 3 cooked lasagna noodles on top of sauce. Spread one-third of cottage cheese mixture on noodles. Top with one-third of sauce mixture, then ½ cup cheese. Repeat layers two times, beginning with noodles and ending with cheese.

7. Bake 25 to 30 minutes or until hot. Remove from oven and let stand 10 minutes before serving.

DIJON FISH WITH SPINACH AND TOMATOES

In this recipe, use any mild-flavored fish such as orange roughy, cod, haddock, halibut, grouper, flounder, sole, snapper, tilapia, or trout.

Makes: 6 servings   Cost per Recipe: $12.95   Cost per Serving: $2.16

¼ cup Dijon mustard

¼ cup reduced-fat Italian dressing

1½ pounds fish fillets (flounder, tilapia, catfish, cod, flounder, trout)

½ cup chopped onion

1 (10-ounce) bag fresh baby spinach (about 6 cups)

1 cup chopped tomato

Nutrition Facts per Serving:

138 Calories; 2.4 g Total Fat (16% from fat); 0.4 g Saturated Fat; 5.4 g Carbohydrates; 22.6 g Protein; 40 mg Cholesterol; 1.6 g Fiber; 304 mg Sodium

1. Preheat broiler. Coat a shallow baking pan with cooking spray or line with foil.

2. Combine mustard and Italian dressing in a small bowl. Arrange fish in prepared pan and brush with half the mustard mixture.

3. Broil fish 5½ inches from heat 8 to 10 minutes or until fish is golden and flakes easily. (Watch carefully to prevent burning.)

4. Combine onion and remaining mustard mixture in a large, nonstick skillet over medium-high heat. Cook, stirring often for 3 to 5 minutes or until onion is tender. Add spinach and tomatoes, and continue to cook until spinach is wilted and tomatoes are tender. Transfer to a serving platter, and arrange fish over spinach mixture.

TIP Fresh and Frozen Fish Safety
When you buy fish fresh from the grocery store, make sure you use it within a day while it's still fresh. Or, purchase frozen fish fillets or steaks and keep them ready to use. Thaw fish in the refrigerator or under cold running water. Never leave fish or any other meat in the sink to thaw at room temperature.

Eat Right for Less

BAKED PARMESAN FISH

It's easy to overcook fish, so watch it carefully. It's done just as soon as the fish reaches 145°F and flakes easily when you test it with a fork.

Makes: 8 servings   Cost per Recipe: $11.55   Cost per Serving: $1.44

2 pounds fish fillets (catfish, flounder, trout, grouper, tilapia)

¼ teaspoon salt

¼ teaspoon pepper

¾ cup fat-free sour cream

2 tablespoons finely chopped onion

½ teaspoon minced garlic

2 tablespoons lemon juice

½ teaspoon hot sauce

⅓ cup grated Parmesan cheese

¼ teaspoon paprika

1. Preheat oven to 350°. Coat a large, shallow baking pan with cooking spray.

2. Season both sides of fish with salt and pepper and place in a single layer in prepared pan. Combine sour cream, onion, garlic, lemon juice, hot sauce, and Parmesan cheese in a small bowl. Spread over fish and let stand 10 minutes. Sprinkle with paprika.

3. Bake 25 minutes or until fish flakes easily with a fork. Serve immediately.

Nutrition Facts per Serving:

144 Calories; 2.6 g Total Fat (16% from fat); 0.9 g Saturated Fat; 4.6 g Carbohydrates; 24.2 g Protein; 61 mg Cholesterol; 0.1 g Fiber; 236 mg Sodium

CURRIED SALMON

Curry powder, a popular seasoning in India, is simply a mixture of 15 or more spices. Turmeric is the spice that gives it the yellow color.

Makes: 4 servings   Cost per Recipe: $6.95   Cost per Serving: $1.74

1 (14½-ounce) can diced tomatoes, undrained

⅔ cup fat-free evaporated milk

1 tablespoon curry powder

¼ teaspoon sugar

¼ teaspoon salt

¼ teaspoon ground ginger

Dash ground cinnamon

1 cup frozen peas and carrots

2 (6- to 7.1-ounce) cans or pouches skinless, boneless salmon, drained

2 cups hot cooked regular or brown rice (cooked without salt or fat); hot, cooked noodles; or four small baked potatoes

1. Combine tomatoes, evaporated milk, curry powder, sugar, salt, ginger and cinnamon in a medium saucepan. Cook over medium heat, stirring often, just until sauce begins to bubble.

2. Stir in peas and carrots; cook 5 minutes.

3. Stir in salmon and cook just until thoroughly heated. Serve with rice, pasta, or baked potatoes.

Nutrition Facts per Serving:

250 Calories; 3.1 g Total Fat (11% from fat); 0.8 g Saturated Fat; 37.9 g Carbohydrates; 17.2 g Protein; 18 mg Cholesterol; 3.1 g Fiber; 568 mg Sodium

TIP Salmon's Good Fat
The omega-3 oils that are found in fatty fish such as salmon are good for your heart. They're so good, in fact, that the American Heart Association recommends eating fish two times a week.

Eat Right for Less

OVEN-ROASTED SALMON WITH CHEDDAR POLENTA

Polenta is a simple Italian side dish made of cornmeal. It's creamy, somewhat like grits or spoonbread. The flavor pairs deliciously with seasoned salmon in this recipe.

Makes: 2 servings   Cost per Recipe: $3.76   Cost per Serving: $1.88

1 teaspoon salt-free lemon-pepper seasoning

2 (4-ounce) salmon fillets

½ medium lemon, sliced

1 teaspoon olive oil

1 (14-ounce) can low-sodium chicken broth

½ teaspoon chopped fresh rosemary or ¼ teaspoon dried crushed rosemary

¼ teaspoon salt

Dash pepper

½ cup finely ground yellow cornmeal

½ cup (2 ounces) shredded 75% reduced-fat cheddar cheese

Nutrition Facts per Serving:

422 Calories; 17.1 g Total Fat (36% calories from fat); 4.4 g Saturated Fat; 31.8 g Carbohydrates; 35 g Protein; 64 mg Cholesterol; 2.9 g Fiber; 606 mg Sodium

1. Preheat oven to 425°. Coat a shallow baking dish with cooking spray.

2. Sprinkle lemon-pepper seasoning over both sides of salmon fillets, and place in prepared baking dish. Top salmon with lemon slices; drizzle with olive oil. Bake 10 minutes or until fish flakes easily when tested with a fork.

3. While salmon bakes, combine chicken broth, rosemary, salt, and pepper in a small saucepan over medium-high heat, and bring to a boil. Gradually whisk in cornmeal, stirring constantly. Reduce heat to medium; cook 2 to 3 minutes or until polenta is thick, stirring frequently. Remove from heat, and stir in cheese.

4. Spoon polenta onto two individual plates. Top with salmon. Serve immediately.

HEARTFELT TUNA MELTS

This hearty, open-face sandwich is perfect with a bowl of tomato soup on a chilly day.

Makes: 4 servings   Cost per Recipe: $5.08   Cost per Serving: $1.27

2 whole-wheat English muffins, split

1 (6-ounce) can or pouch solid white tuna packed in water, drained

⅓ cup chopped celery

¼ cup chopped onion

¼ cup fat-free Thousand Island dressing or low-fat Russian dressing

¼ teaspoon salt

¼ teaspoon pepper

¾ cup (3 ounces) shredded 75% reduced-fat cheddar cheese

1. Preheat broiler. Place English muffins split-side up on baking sheet; set under broiler until lightly toasted.

2. Combine tuna, celery, onion, salad dressing, salt, and pepper in a medium bowl. Top each toasted muffin half with one-fourth of tuna mixture. Return to broiler until heated through, about 2 to 3 minutes.

3. Top each with one-fourth of the cheese and return to broiler until cheese is melted, about 1 minute.

Nutrition Facts per Serving:

188 Calories; 5.3 g Total Fat (25% from fat); 2.6 g Saturated Fat; 17.9 g Carbohydrates; 18.4 g Protein; 28 mg Cholesterol; 2.3 g Fiber; 658 mg Sodium

TIP What's in a Can of Tuna?

Albacore tuna is a white, flaky fish fillet. You'll have to break it apart with a fork to add it to a recipe. It's a little more expensive, but not as "fishy" tasting as other types. Chunk light tuna is chopped tuna. Be sure to get tuna packed in water rather than in oil to save fat and calories. Also, note that cans of tuna and salmon usually are cheaper than the handy rip-open pouches.

Eat Right for Less

CREAMY TUNA-PASTA DINNER

This recipe works with chopped, cooked chicken or turkey, also. Just substitute 1½ cups of chicken or turkey for the can of tuna. If you don't have the corkscrew-shaped rotini pasta, then use elbow or shell macaroni instead.

Makes: 6 servings   Cost per Recipe: $7.02   Cost per Serving: $1.17

2 cups whole-wheat or regular rotini pasta, uncooked

1 (14½-ounce) can peas and carrots, drained, or 1½ cups frozen peas and carrots, thawed

1 (12-ounce) can albacore tuna packed in water, drained

1 tablespoon butter or margarine

2 tablespoons all-purpose flour

1½ cups fat-free evaporated milk

1 (8-ounce) package fat-free cream cheese, softened

1 teaspoon garlic powder

¼ teaspoon salt

½ teaspoon pepper

1. Cook pasta according to package directions in a large saucepan or Dutch oven. Drain and return cooked pasta to saucepan. Stir in peas and carrots, and tuna.

2. Melt butter in a medium saucepan over medium heat. Add flour, stirring constantly, until combined. (Mixture will be lumpy.) Gradually add evaporated milk, stirring constantly with a whisk until smooth. Stir in cream cheese, mixing until smooth. Remove from heat and stir in garlic powder, salt, and pepper.

3. Pour sauce over cooked pasta mixture, stirring gently. Serve immediately.

Nutrition Facts per Serving:

264 Calories; 4.4 g Total Fat (15% calories from fat); 2.0 g Saturated Fat; 31.0 g Carbohydrates; 24.6 g Protein; 33 mg Cholesterol; 1.7 g Fiber; 698 mg Sodium

SIDES/SALADS

** If no external source is listed in parentheses for a recipe,
the recipe was developed by the authors.*

LAYERED MEXICAN SALAD

If you're having a few friends over, this is a great salad to serve as an appetizer. With a meal, serve it with chicken chili or a hot soup.

Makes: 8 servings   Cost per Recipe: $7.45   Cost per Serving: $0.93

4 cups shredded or torn lettuce

1 cup chopped red onion

1 (16-ounce) can reduced-sodium dark red kidney beans, drained

1 cup chopped fresh tomato

½ cup light mayonnaise

½ cup fat-free sour cream

1 teaspoon lime juice

½ cup salsa

1½ cups (6 ounces) shredded 75% reduced-fat cheddar cheese

1 (2¼-ounce) can sliced black olives, drained

1. Arrange lettuce in bottom of a shallow 2-quart dish. Sprinkle onion evenly over lettuce. Layer kidney beans evenly over onion. Layer chopped tomato over beans.

2. Combine mayonnaise, sour cream, lime juice, and salsa in a small bowl. Spread evenly over top of salad. Cover and refrigerate.

3. Just before serving, arrange cheese and olives on top.

Nutrition Facts per Serving:

144 Calories; 4.8 g Total Fat (30% calories from fat); 1.8 g Saturated Fat; 16.1 g Carbohydrates; 10.7 g Protein; 10 mg Cholesterol; 4.8 g Fiber; 479 mg Sodium

SALSA REFRIED BEANS

If you don't use reduced-sodium pinto beans, this recipe will be high in sodium. If sodium is an issue in your diet, you can reduce it even more by cooking dried beans yourself.

Makes: 4 servings   Cost per Recipe: $2.40   Cost per Serving: $0.60

2 (16-ounce) cans reduced-sodium pinto beans, undrained

½ cup salsa

¼ teaspoon ground cumin

½ cup (2 ounces) shredded 50% reduced-fat cheddar cheese

Nutrition Facts per Serving:

196 Calories; 2.3 g Total Fat (11% calories from fat); 1.5 g Saturated Fat; 35.6 g Carbohydrates; 15.5 g Protein; 8 mg Cholesterol; 12.3 g Fiber; 314 mg Sodium

1. Pour beans into a nonstick skillet and place over medium heat. Cook 5 minutes until beans are hot, stirring often to prevent sticking. Using the back of a wooden spoon, mash beans in skillet until they stick together.

2. Stir in salsa and cumin. Cook 1 minute, stirring often, until mixture is thoroughly heated.

3. Transfer bean mixture to a shallow 1½-quart dish. Immediately sprinkle cheese over beans. Cover with aluminum foil and let stand a few minutes just until cheese melts.

TIP Cooking Dried Beans

Cooking dried beans is the best way to control the amount of fat and salt in the beans. Here's how: rinse 1 pound of dried beans and discard any foreign particles or shriveled beans. Place the beans in a Dutch oven or a large, heavy saucepan. Add water to cover the beans 2 inches, and soak them at least 8 hours. Drain. Add 2 quarts of water and seasonings. (Wait to add salt until after the beans are cooked, or they can be tough and take longer to cook.) Bring the water to a boil over high heat, then reduce the heat to low and simmer 2 hours. Drain. The beans are ready to eat or use in recipes.

Eat Right for Less

BROCCOLI-RICE CASSEROLE

For a little more flavor kick, use 50% reduced-fat pepper jack or jalapeno cheddar cheese instead of regular cheddar cheese. If you don't have fresh mushrooms, just stir in mushrooms from a jar or can, or leave them out.

Makes: 6 servings   Cost per Recipe: $4.09   Cost per Serving: $0.68

½ cup sliced fresh mushrooms

½ cup chopped red bell pepper

¼ cup chopped onion

1 (10-ounce) package chopped frozen broccoli, thawed

2 cups cooked regular or brown rice (cooked without salt or fat)

1 large egg

½ cup fat-free evaporated milk

½ teaspoon salt

½ teaspoon pepper

¾ cup (3 ounces) shredded, 50% reduced-fat cheddar cheese

Nutrition Facts per Serving:

158 Calories; 3.7 g Total Fat (21% calories from fat); 1.8 g Saturated Fat; 22.1 g Carbohydrates; 9.9 g Protein; 43 mg Cholesterol; 2.4 g Fiber; 331 mg Sodium

1. Preheat oven to 375°. Coat a 2-quart baking dish with cooking spray.

2. Combine mushrooms, bell pepper, and onion in a large microwave-safe bowl. Add 1 tablespoon water to bowl; cover with plastic wrap and cook on HIGH 2 minutes or until vegetables are soft. Drain. Stir in broccoli and rice.

3. Add egg, milk, salt, and pepper to broccoli mixture, stirring well.

4. Spoon broccoli-rice mixture into the prepared baking dish. Sprinkle with cheese. Bake 25 minutes. Serve hot.

TIP Which Bell Pepper to Use?

Red, orange, yellow, and green bell peppers come from the same plant, but are just picked at different stages of ripeness. Besides color, they differ in taste and price. Usually, riper red bell peppers are more expensive, but have a sweeter flavor and add nice color to casseroles and salads. Farmers' markets often are a great place to buy peppers and other produce—it's fresher from the farm and cheaper, too.

FRUITED COLESLAW

This coleslaw tastes even better the day after you make it. Prepare it a day before you serve it to give the flavors time to blend.

Makes: 6 servings   Cost per Recipe: $3.58   Cost per Serving: $0.60

½ cup light mayonnaise

¼ cup sugar

2 tablespoons cider vinegar

½ teaspoon salt

½ teaspoon dry mustard

⅛ teaspoon celery seeds

4 cups shredded cabbage

1 cup shredded carrot

1 (8-ounce) can crushed pineapple, undrained

½ cup raisins

1. Combine mayonnaise, sugar, vinegar, salt, mustard, and celery seeds in a large bowl.

2. Stir in cabbage, carrot, pineapple, and raisins, mixing well. Cover and refrigerate.

Nutrition Facts per Serving:

146 Calories; 2.9 g Total Fat (18% calories from fat); 0.7 g Saturated Fat; 30.7 g Carbohydrates; 1.6 g Protein; 146 mg Cholesterol; 2.4 g Fiber; 393 mg Sodium

Eat Right for Less

HONEYED CARROT SALAD

This recipe is perfect for picnics and packed lunches, as well as for lunch or dinner. If you don't have chopped dates, substitute raisins. You'll find it tastes better if you use freshly shredded carrots instead of the packaged pre-grated carrots. You'll also save money by shredding the carrots yourself.

Makes: 4 servings   Cost per Recipe: $3.58   Cost per Serving: $0.90

3 cups finely shredded carrots

1 cup finely chopped, unpeeled apple

¼ cup chopped dates

¼ cup light mayonnaise

2 teaspoons honey

½ teaspoon ground cinnamon

1. Combine carrots, apple, and dates in a large bowl.

2. Combine mayonnaise, honey, and cinnamon in a small bowl. Add mayonnaise mixture to carrot mixture, stirring well. Cover and refrigerate.

Nutrition Facts per Serving:

117 Calories; 2.3 g Total Fat (2% calories from fat); 0.5 g Saturated Fat; 25.4 g Carbohydrates; 1.1 g Protein; 0 mg Cholesterol; 4.0 g Fiber; 187 mg Sodium

TIP Keep the Peel

Any time you use fresh vegetables or fruit as a snack or in cooking, it's healthier to leave the peel on. The peel provides extra fiber and valuable nutrients. Be sure to wash all vegetables and fruit before you eat them to avoid possible food-borne illness.

HERBED ROASTED POTATOES

Cutting the potatoes extremely thin and roasting them in a single layer at a very high temperature are the tricks to crispy potato slices.

Makes: 6 servings   Cost per Recipe: $0.68   Cost per Serving: $0.11

1 pound unpeeled potatoes, scrubbed and thinly sliced

½ teaspoon olive oil

2 tablespoons Italian seasoning

½ teaspoon garlic powder

½ teaspoon salt

¼ teaspoon pepper

Nutrition Facts per Serving:

81 Calories; 0.7 g Total Fat (8% calories from fat); 0.1 g Saturated Fat; 16.9 g Carbohydrates; 1.9 g Protein; 0 mg Cholesterol; 2.1 g Fiber; 200 mg Sodium

1. Preheat oven to 475°. Coat a 15 x 10-inch baking pan with cooking spray.

2. Place potato slices in a large, zip-top plastic bag. Add olive oil, seal bag, and gently turn bag back and forth to coat potatoes.

3. Add Italian seasoning, garlic powder, salt, and pepper to zip-top bag with potatoes. Seal the bag and gently turn the bag back and forth until potatoes are evenly coated with seasonings.

4. Arrange potatoes in a single layer in the prepared pan. Bake 10 minutes. Turn potato slices with a spatula, and bake 10 minutes longer or until golden brown.

Eat Right for Less

ORANGE SWEET POTATOES

To dress this recipe up for the holidays, cut three oranges in half and scrape out the pulp to use for a fruit salad. Spoon the sweet potato mixture into the orange shells and bake.

Make: 6 servings   Cost per Recipe: $5.39   Cost per Serving: $0.90

1 (11-ounce) can mandarin oranges in light syrup, drained

3 cups cooked, mashed sweet potato

½ cup orange juice

2 tablespoons light brown sugar

1 teaspoon vanilla extract

½ teaspoon ground cinnamon

⅓ cup chopped pecans

Nutrition Facts per Serving:

221 Calories; 5.1 g Total Fat (21% calories from fat); 0.5 g Saturated Fat; 41.9 g Carbohydrates; 3.4 g Protein; 0 mg Cholesterol; 5.1 g Fiber; 50 mg Sodium

1. Preheat oven to 350°. Coat a 1½-quart baking dish with cooking spray.

2. Coarsely chop mandarin oranges and place in a bowl. Add sweet potato, orange juice, brown sugar, vanilla, and cinnamon to oranges, mixing well.

3. Spoon sweet potato mixture into prepared dish and sprinkle pecans on top. Bake 25 minutes. Serve hot.

TIP Sweet Potato or Yam?
Sweet potatoes are sometimes called yams, which you may have seen on can labels in the supermarket. Look for darker-skinned sweet potatoes with smooth, unbruised skins.

SPINACH SALAD WITH FETA CHEESE

Even if you buy packaged spinach leaves that indicate they have been "pre-washed," be sure to wash the leaves anyway, to reduce the possibility of illness from bacteria that may be on the leaves.

Makes: 4 servings   Cost per Recipe: $2.26   Cost per Serving: $0.57

4 cups fresh, baby spinach leaves

½ cup chopped, unpeeled red apple

¼ cup dried cranberries or raisins

2 tablespoons crumbled, reduced-fat feta cheese

½ cup fat-free balsamic or raspberry vinaigrette dressing

1. In a large bowl, toss spinach, apple, and cranberries.

2. Divide mixture evenly in four individual salad bowls. Top each with feta cheese and 2 tablespoons balsamic vinaigrette.

Nutrition Facts per Serving:

58 Calories; 0.5 g Total Fat (8% calories from fat); 0.4 g Saturated Fat; 12.0 g Carbohydrates; 2.5 g Protein; 2 mg Cholesterol; 1.9 g Fiber; 239 mg Sodium

Eat Right for Less

SQUASH AND TOMATO SKILLET STIR-FRY

Be sure to cook the squash just until it's crisp-tender for the best flavor and texture; don't over-cook it. Zucchini can be substituted for the yellow squash, or you can use half of each.

Makes: 6 servings   Cost per Recipe: $4.30   Cost per Serving: $0.72

2 slices turkey bacon

½ teaspoon olive oil

1 teaspoon minced garlic

1 cup sliced onion

4 cups sliced yellow squash (about 4 medium)

1½ cups chopped tomatoes

2 tablespoons chopped fresh oregano or 2 teaspoons dried oregano

¼ teaspoon salt

¼ teaspoon pepper

Nutrition Facts per Serving:

45 Calories; 1.3 g Total Fat (26% calories from fat); 0.3 g Saturated Fat; 6.8 g Carbohydrates; 2.2 g Protein; 3 mg Cholesterol; 1.6 g Fiber; 148 mg Sodium

1. Place a nonstick skillet over medium-high heat. Add turkey bacon, and cook 1 to 2 minutes on each side or until browned. Remove from skillet and chop bacon.

2. Add olive oil to hot skillet. Add garlic and onion to skillet, and cook, stirring constantly, 1 minute. Add squash and cook 5 minutes, stirring constantly, until squash is browned and crisp-tender.

3. Stir in tomatoes, oregano, salt, pepper, and bacon; cook 1 minute or until tomato is thoroughly heated. Serve hot.

GARDEN PASTA SALAD

This recipe is ideal for a brown bag lunch, for a potluck dinner, or to keep in the fridge and have on-hand. And if you don't need such a large quantity, simply prepare half of the recipe. It uses tri-color pasta, which is actually made from beets, tomato, and spinach. Or, you can substitute whole-wheat rotini, elbow macaroni, or penne pasta.

Makes: 12 servings   Cost per Recipe: $8.62   Cost per Serving: $0.72

16 ounces uncooked tri-color rotini pasta

1 cup light mayonnaise

⅓ cup lemon juice

2 tablespoons sugar

2 tablespoons Dijon mustard

1 tablespoon chopped fresh basil or 1 teaspoon dried basil leaves

1 teaspoon salt

1 cup chopped broccoli flowerets

1 cup sliced carrot

1 cup coarsely chopped red bell pepper

1 cup chopped red onion

1 cup coarsely chopped zucchini

Nutrition Facts per Serving:

195 Calories; 3.7 g Total Fat (17% calories from fat); 0.2 g Saturated Fat; 38.0 g Carbohydrates; 6.0 g Protein; 0 mg Cholesterol; 2.4 g Fiber; 438 mg Sodium

1. Cook pasta according to package directions. Drain.

2. Combine mayonnaise, lemon juice, sugar, mustard, basil, and salt in a large bowl. Add cooked pasta to mayonnaise mixture.

3. Stir in broccoli, carrot, bell pepper, onion, and zucchini. Serve warm, or cover and refrigerate.

TIP Good-for-You Whole-Wheat Pasta

As a good source of fiber, B vitamins, and other nutrients, three servings of whole grains a day is recommended by the USDA. Whole-grain pastas are a good way to meet that goal. Research says eating whole-wheat products may lower the risk of heart disease, cancer, diabetes, and obesity.

Eat Right for Less

CREAMY MAC & CHEESE

This macaroni-and-cheese recipe is made healthier by using fat-free or reduced-fat products to save on calories and fat, and whole-wheat pasta, which provides fiber and extra nutrients. A good tip for the best pasta: stir often to keep the pasta moving as it cooks.

Makes: 8 servings   Cost per Recipe: $3.54   Cost per Serving: $0.44

3 cups uncooked, whole-wheat or regular elbow macaroni

1 tablespoon butter or margarine

2 tablespoons all-purpose flour

1 (12-ounce) can fat-free, evaporated milk

½ teaspoon salt

1 cup (4 ounces) shredded 50% reduced-fat cheddar cheese

¼ cup fat-free cream cheese

Nutrition Facts per Serving:

234 Calories; 4.3 g Total Fat (17% calories from fat); 2.6 g Saturated Fat; 15.4 g Carbohydrates; 13.9 g Protein; 15 mg Cholesterol; 3.3 g Fiber; 340 mg Sodium

1. Cook macaroni according to package directions. Drain.

2. While macaroni cooks, melt butter in a large saucepan over medium heat. Add flour, stirring constantly with a wooden spoon or a whisk. (Mixture will be lumpy.) Gradually add evaporated milk, stirring constantly. Continue to cook, stirring constantly, until mixture is smooth. Stir in salt and cheese. Remove from heat and add cream cheese, stirring until smooth.

3. Add cooked macaroni to cheese sauce, mixing well. Serve hot.

LEMONY BROWN RICE

Brown rice takes longer to cook than white rice. It needs 40 to 45 minutes on the stovetop instead of the typical 20 minutes for white rice. Besides the health benefits, brown rice offers a chewy, nut-like flavor. For extra flavor, stir in fresh or dried herbs.

Makes: 4 servings   Cost per Recipe: $1.68   Cost per Serving: $0.42

2½ cups fat-free chicken broth

¼ cup lemon juice

½ teaspoon grated lemon zest

½ teaspoon salt

1 cup uncooked brown rice

Nutrition Facts per Serving with Brown Rice:

178 Calories; 1.4 g Total Fat (2% calories from fat); 0.3 g Saturated Fat; 36.6 g Carbohydrates; 4.7 g Protein; 0 mg Cholesterol; 2.9 g Fiber; 583 mg Sodium

1. Combine broth, lemon juice, lemon rind, and salt in a 2-quart saucepan; bring to a boil over medium-high heat.

2. Stir in rice. Reduce heat to low; cover with lid and cook 40 minutes or until rice is tender and liquid is absorbed. Serve hot.

TIP About Brown Rice

Brown rice is simply white rice without the bran or germ removed, which makes it a whole-grain product and extra good for you. One-half cup of brown rice is equal to one of the three recommended daily servings of whole grains. You can keep dry rice at room temperature up to 6 months, but if you plan to store it longer, put it in the refrigerator or freezer so it will stay fresh.

DESSERTS

** If no external source is listed in parentheses for a recipe,
the recipe was developed by the authors.*

LAYERED PEANUT BUTTER-CHOCOLATE PARFAITS

QUICK & EASY · KID FRIENDLY

You don't have to have a tall, skinny parfait glass to make this dessert. A drinking glass, or even an individual cereal or salad bowl, will work just fine. Clear glasses allow the pretty layers to show.

Makes: 6 servings   Cost per Recipe: $3.01   Cost per Serving: $ 0.50

2 cups fat-free milk

¼ cup reduced-fat, crunchy peanut butter

1 (3.3-ounce) box white chocolate instant pudding and pie filling mix

1 cup crushed chocolate sandwich cookies, divided

1 cup fat-free frozen whipped topping, thawed

Nutrition Facts per Serving:

314 Calories; 10.2 g Total Fat (29% calories from fat); 2.3 g Saturated Fat; 50.1 g Carbohydrates; 6.8 g Protein; 2 mg Cholesterol; 1.6 g Fiber; 483 mg Sodium

1. Combine milk and peanut butter in a large bowl, stirring with a wooden spoon or a whisk to mix. Stir in pudding mix, mixing well. Let stand 5 minutes or until pudding thickens.

2. Reserve 1 tablespoon crushed cookies for garnish. Spoon half the pudding evenly into the bottom of six parfait or other tall glasses. Sprinkle half the remaining crushed cookies over pudding. Top with half the whipped topping. Repeat layers, ending with whipped topping. To garnish, top each serving with ½ teaspoon of the reserved crushed cookies.

Eat Right for Less

CHOCOLATE CHERRY TRIFLE

This dessert is delicious served right away, but the longer you allow it to chill the more flavorful it will be.

Makes: 12 servings   Cost per Recipe: $8.58   Cost per Serving: $0.72

1 (3.9-ounce) box chocolate instant pudding and pie filling mix

2 cups fat-free milk

¼ cup sliced almonds, toasted

1 (8-ounce) angel food cake

1 (16-ounce) package frozen, no-sugar-added, pitted, dark sweet cherries, thawed

¼ teaspoon almond extract

2 cups fat-free, frozen, whipped topping, thawed

1 tablespoon grated, semisweet chocolate

Nutrition Facts per Serving:

156 Calories; 1.7 g Total Fat (10% calories from fat); 0.4 g Saturated Fat; 31.9 g Carbohydrates; 3.7 g Protein; 1 mg Cholesterol; 1.8 g Fiber; 198 mg Sodium

1. Prepare pudding mix in a medium bowl according to package directions, using the fat-free milk. When pudding begins to thicken, stir in almonds.

2. Cut or tear angel food cake into 2-inch cubes. Place half the cake cubes in a 3-quart, deep, glass dish or bowl.

3. Combine cherries and almond extract in a bowl. Spoon half the cherry mixture over cake in glass dish. Spread half the pudding over cherries, and top with half the whipped topping. Repeat layers. Top with grated chocolate. Cover and refrigerate at least 1 hour before serving.

TIP Toast Nuts for Extra Flavor

Toasting nuts gives them a stronger flavor. Just spread the nuts in a single layer in a microwave-safe dish, and microwave on HIGH for 30 seconds. Stir. Microwave 30 seconds longer or until the nuts taste toasted and are lightly browned.

CREAMY FROZEN FRUIT DESSERT

This recipe is a good one for taking to potluck dinners or when you need to feed a crowd. Or, you can spoon it into two smaller dishes to freeze; you'll have one to serve the family and have a spare for later. If you prefer to cut the recipe in half, it won't hurt to stir in the whole can of pineapple tidbits in the halved version.

Makes: 15 servings   Cost per Recipe: $9.94   Cost per Serving: $0.66

1 (8-ounce) package fat-free cream cheese, softened

½ cup sugar

1 (8-ounce) can pineapple tidbits in juice, drained

2 cups fresh or frozen blueberries

1 cup fresh or frozen unsweetened strawberries, thawed

2 cups sliced ripe bananas (about two large)

⅓ cup chopped pecans, toasted

1 (16-ounce) carton fat-free, frozen, whipped topping, thawed

1. Beat cream cheese in a large bowl on the high speed of an electric mixer until fluffy. Gradually add sugar, beating until smooth.

2. Stir in pineapple, blueberries, strawberries, bananas, and pecans. Fold in whipped topping.

3. Pour mixture into a 13 x 9-inch freezer-safe dish. Cover and freeze at least 8 hours. Let stand 10 minutes at room temperature to soften before serving. Cut into squares.

Nutrition Facts per Serving:

151 Calories; 2.3 g Total Fat (14% calories from fat); 0.3 g Saturated Fat; 28.8 g Carbohydrates; 2.9 g Protein; 1 mg Cholesterol; 1.7 g Fiber; 100 mg Sodium

Eat Right for Less

ORANGE-SPICED BANANAS WITH ICE CREAM

You'll get a much stronger orange flavor if you use juice and zest from a fresh orange in this recipe. Zest is the colored, flavorful outer layer of the rind. Try to avoid grating into the white layer under the zest, since it has a bitter taste. If you don't have an orange, just skip the zest and use orange juice you have on hand.

Makes: 6 servings   Cost per Recipe: $2.24   Cost per Serving: $0.37

2 teaspoons butter or margarine

1 teaspoon grated orange zest

¼ cup orange juice

2 tablespoons light brown sugar

¼ teaspoon ground cinnamon

½ teaspoon vanilla extract

2 cups sliced, ripe bananas
(about two large)

3 cups fat-free, vanilla ice cream

Nutrition Facts per Serving:

163 Calories; 1.5 g Total Fat (8% calories from fat); 0.9 g Saturated Fat; 36.6 g Carbohydrates; 3.6 g Protein; 3 mg Cholesterol; 4.4 g Fiber; 61 mg Sodium

1. Add butter to non-stick skillet and place over medium heat until melted. Stir in orange zest, orange juice, brown sugar, and cinnamon. Cook, stirring constantly, 1 minute or until sugar dissolves. Stir in vanilla.

2. Add bananas to skillet and cook over medium-high heat for 2 minutes or until thoroughly heated, stirring to coat banana slices.

3. Spoon ½ cup ice cream in each of six serving bowls. Spoon banana mixture evenly over ice cream.

WARM PEACH CRISP

Fresh fruit is at its sweetest when it is in season, so substitute other fruit for peaches depending on the time of year. In summer, use peaches, blueberries, or blackberries. In fall months, make this crisp with apples or pears.

Makes: 6 servings   Cost per Recipe: $4.25   Cost per Serving: $0.71

6 cups peeled, sliced fresh or frozen peaches

½ teaspoon grated lemon zest

2 tablespoons lemon juice

⅓ cup old-fashioned quick oats, uncooked

⅓ cup firmly packed, light-brown sugar

¼ cup all-purpose flour

½ teaspoon ground cinnamon

½ teaspoon ground nutmeg

⅛ teaspoon salt

2 tablespoons cold butter or margarine

1½ cups low-fat vanilla frozen yogurt

1. Preheat oven to 375°. Spoon peaches into an 8-inch baking pan or dish coated with cooking spray. Sprinkle lemon zest and lemon juice over peaches.

2. Combine oats, brown sugar, flour, cinnamon, nutmeg, and salt in a small bowl, stirring well. Add butter to oat mixture, and using two knives or a pastry blender, cut in butter until crumbly. Sprinkle over fruit mixture.

3. Bake 35 to 40 minutes or until peaches are tender and topping is golden brown. Spoon warm peach crisp into serving bowls and top with frozen yogurt.

Nutrition Facts per Serving:

236 Calories; 5.4 g Total Fat (21% calories from fat); 3.0 g Saturated Fat; 44.2 g Carbohydrates; 5.8 g Protein; 13 mg Cholesterol; 3.3 g Fiber; 122 mg Sodium

TIP "Cutting In" Cold Butter

A pastry blender is a handy tool to use when you need to cut cold butter into tiny pieces to mix with dry ingredients. Just rock it back and forth in the bowl until the butter pieces are the size of small peas. Instead of a pastry blender, you can use two knives. Hold one in each hand and pull them toward each other, cutting through the butter like scissors.

Eat Right for Less

LUSCIOUS LEMON CUPCAKES

Most of the fat in eggs is in the yolks, so using just egg whites in this recipe keeps the fat lower and gives the cupcakes a light texture like sponge cake. You'll get a stronger lemon flavor if you use fresh lemon juice.

Makes: 20 cupcakes   Cost per Recipe: $2.75   Cost per Cupcake: $0.14

½ cup butter or margarine, softened

1½ cups sugar

1¾ cups all-purpose flour

2½ teaspoons baking powder

½ teaspoon salt

1 teaspoon grated lemon zest

⅔ cup fat-free milk

¼ cup lemon juice

1 teaspoon vanilla extract

4 large egg whites

1 teaspoon powdered sugar

Nutrition Facts per Serving:

149 Calories; 5.0 g Total Fat (30% calories from fat); 2.9 g Saturated Fat; 24.3 g Carbohydrates; 2.2 g Protein; 12 mg Cholesterol; 0.3 g Fiber; 167 mg Sodium

TIP Get More Lemon Juice
When you are using juice from a fresh lemon, lime, or orange, always grate the zest first. To extract the most juice, place the fruit in the microwave oven and microwave it on HIGH 15 to 20 seconds. Then, roll it on the counter, pressing firmly with your hand before cutting it in half to squeeze out the juice.

1. Preheat oven to 350°. Place paper cupcake liners in muffin pans. Coat cupcake liners with cooking spray.

2. Beat butter in a large bowl at medium speed of an electric mixer until creamy; gradually add sugar, beating well.

3. Combine flour, baking powder, salt, and lemon zest in a small bowl. Combine milk and lemon juice in a small bowl. Add flour mixture to butter mixture alternately with milk mixture, beginning and ending with flour mixture. Mix well after each addition. Stir in vanilla.

4. Beat egg whites at high speed of electric mixture until stiff peaks form. (Make sure beaters are clean and dry.) Fold beaten egg whites into batter. Spoon batter into prepared cupcake liners.

5. Bake 20 minutes or until a wooden pick inserted in center of a cupcake comes out clean. Remove from oven and cool in pans on wire racks 10 minutes. Remove cupcakes from pans to wire rack and cool completely. Sift powdered sugar over tops of cooled cupcakes.

EASY NO-CRUST PUMPKIN PIE

Pumpkin, which is actually a type of squash, is packed with Vitamin A. So if your kids won't eat orange or yellow vegetables, this dessert is a good way to sneak more nutrients into their diet. If you want to make this recipe look fancier for the holidays or for a special occasion, spoon dollops of fat-free whipped topping around the edges and top each one with a pecan half.

Makes: 8 servings   Cost per Recipe: $2.45   Cost per Serving: $0.31

2 large eggs

1 (16-ounce) can pumpkin or 2 cups cooked, mashed pumpkin or sweet potato

1 cup fat-free, evaporated milk

⅔ cup firmly packed brown sugar

¼ cup all-purpose flour

1 teaspoon ground cinnamon

½ teaspoon ground ginger

¼ teaspoon ground nutmeg

¼ teaspoon salt

Nutrition Facts per Serving:

149 Calories; 1.6 g Total Fat (10% calories from fat); 0.5 g Saturated Fat; 29.9 g Carbohydrates; 4.6 g Protein; 55 mg Cholesterol; 1.9 g Fiber; 140 mg Sodium

1. Preheat oven to 350°. Coat a 9-inch pie plate with cooking spray.

2. Beat eggs in a large bowl. Add pumpkin, evaporated milk, brown sugar, flour, cinnamon, ginger, nutmeg, and salt, mixing well. Pour mixture into prepared pie plate.

3. Bake 45 minutes or until a knife inserted in the center comes out clean. Remove from oven and cool on a wire rack at least 10 minutes before serving.

Eat Right for Less

CHEWY OATMEAL CHOCOLATE CHIP COOKIES

MAKE AHEAD

KID FRIENDLY

Unsweetened applesauce replaces the butter in this recipe to make delicious, but low-fat cookies. Using applesauce makes the cookies stay chewy and moist. For variations, substitute raisins, dried cranberries, pecans, or walnuts for chocolate chips.

Makes: 2½ dozen cookies   Cost per Recipe: $2.58   Cost per Cookie: $0.09

1¼ cups old-fashioned or quick oats, uncooked

1¼ cups all-purpose flour

½ teaspoon baking soda

½ teaspoon salt

1 teaspoon ground nutmeg

2 large egg whites

¾ cup firmly packed brown sugar

½ cup unsweetened applesauce

1 teaspoon vanilla extract

½ cup semi-sweet chocolate chips

Nutrition Facts per Serving (with chocolate chips):

70 Calories; 1.3 g Total Fat (17% calories from fat); 0.5 g Saturated Fat; 13.9 g Carbohydrates; 1.4 g Protein; 0 mg Cholesterol; 0.7 g Fiber; 66 mg Sodium

1. Preheat oven to 350°. Coat a baking sheet with cooking spray.

2. Combine oats, flour, baking soda, salt, and nutmeg in a medium bowl.

4. Beat egg whites in a large bowl. Add brown sugar, applesauce, and vanilla, mixing well. Stir oat mixture into egg white mixture. Stir in chocolate chips.

5. Drop dough by heaping teaspoonfuls onto prepared baking sheet. Bake 10 minutes or until edges are lightly browned. Cool on baking sheet 2 minutes; transfer cookies to a wire rack and cool completely.

SNACKS

PB&J ROLL-UPS

Children will love these rolled-up peanut butter and jelly sandwiches; they're easy for little hands to hold. For flavor variety, substitute honey, apple butter, or jam for jelly.

Makes: 4 servings   Cost per Recipe: $0.96   Cost per Serving: $0.24

⅓ cup reduced-fat or regular peanut butter

⅓ cup grape or apple jelly

4 slices whole wheat bread

Nutrition Facts per Sandwich:

244 Calories; 8.3 g Total Fat (31% calories from fat); 1.5 g Saturated Fat; 37.2 g Carbohydrates; 8.6 g Protein; 0 mg Cholesterol; 3.3 g Fiber; 266 mg Sodium

1. Combine peanut butter and jelly in a small bowl.

2. Using a rolling pin, clean heavy can, or drinking glass, roll out each bread slice as thin as possible.

3. Spread one side of each slice of bread with peanut butter mixture. Begin at one end of bread and roll up tightly.

TIP Go Whole Grain When You Can
Whole grain or multi-grain bread slices, English muffins, pita pockets, tortillas, and pasta give you extra fiber and other beneficial nutrients needed for a healthy diet. If you have white bread fans at your house, look for the new whole wheat "white" bread slices.

PEAR BOATS

For younger children, peel fresh pears or use canned halves. Fruit skins can be hard for them to swallow.

Makes: 2 servings   Cost per recipe: $0.89   Cost per serving: $0.45

1 ripe pear, halved, or 2 canned pear halves, blotted dry

¼ cup shredded, 50% reduced-fat cheddar cheese

2 tablespoons dried raisins or cranberries

1 teaspoon reduced-fat mayonnaise

1. Scoop out the center core of each pear half (if using a fresh pear) with a spoon.

2. Combine cheese, raisins, and mayonnaise in a small bowl. Fill pear half centers with cheese mixture.

Nutrition Facts per Serving:

114 Calories; 2.7 g Total Fat (21% calories from fat); 1.5 g Saturated Fat; 20.4 g Carbohydrates; 4.6 g Protein; 8 mg Cholesterol; 2.9 g Fiber; 108 mg Sodium

TIP Protein Power

High-protein foods like nuts, cheese, beans, and meat help you feel more satisfied, so you're not as likely to keep snacking on high-calorie food. Any snack with cheese or peanut butter helps to curb kids' hunger until you are ready to serve supper.

Eat Right for Less

SURPRISE-FILLED APPLES

Take this snack in the car or on a hike, or pack it in a lunch box. It's eco-friendly—no wrapper or package to throw away.

Makes: 2 servings   Cost per Recipe: $1.48   Cost per Serving: $0.74

2 small unpeeled apples

3 tablespoons reduced-fat or regular peanut butter

1 tablespoon mashed banana

1 teaspoon raisins

Nutrition Facts per Serving:

180 Calories; 8.2 g Total Fat (41% calories from fat); 1.5 g Saturated Fat; 23.3 g Carbohydrates; 7.0 g Protein; 0 mg Cholesterol; 4.0 g Fiber; 135 mg Sodium

1. Slice off the top third of each apple and set aside. Remove seeds and core from bottom halves of apples, and hollow out centers using a spoon.

2. Combine peanut butter, banana, and raisins in a small bowl. Spoon peanut butter mixture into hollowed-out apples. Replace apple tops.

TIP Fast, Fun Snack Idea
Core an apple or pear and then slice it horizontally so each slice looks like a doughnut. Kids will love poking fingers through the holes and eating the fruit "rings." Leave the peel on the fruit for extra fiber (except when preparing apples for small children who might choke on the peel).

FRUIT DUNKS

The ideal diet includes three servings a day of low-fat dairy foods and two or more servings of fruits. This recipe helps you meet both goals.

Makes: 2 servings   Cost per recipe: $1.33   Cost per serving: $0.67

½ cup low-fat vanilla or lemon yogurt, divided

16 red or green seedless grapes

8 (1-inch) slices banana (1 small)

10 (1-inch) chunks canned or fresh pineapple

1. Spoon ¼ cup yogurt into small individual bowls and set each on a small plate.

2. Spear fruit on toothpicks and divide between plates for dipping.

Nutrition Facts per Serving:

149 Calories; 1.1 g Total Fat (7% calories from fat); 0.6 g Saturated Fat; 33.8 g Carbohydrates; 4.1 g Protein; 3 mg Cholesterol; 2.4 g Fiber; 42 mg Sodium

TIP Eat More Calcium

Look for ways to add more calcium to your diet with low-fat dairy products. Add dry milk powder to casseroles and soups; serve low-fat frozen yogurt for dessert; mix fat-free yogurt with honey for dipping fruit; and keep slices, cubes, or sticks of cheese in zip-top plastic bags in the refrigerator for easy snacking.

EASY PEACH SALSA

You probably have everything you need on hand to make this sweet-hot salsa, so you can whip it up in 5 minutes or less. In summer months, use sweet fresh peaches instead of canned.

Makes: 6 servings   Cost per Recipe: $1.67   Cost per Serving: $0.29

1 cup salsa

½ cup chopped fresh or canned peaches

2 tablespoons chopped green onion

1 teaspoon lime juice

1 teaspoon honey

Baked tortilla chips

1. Combine salsa, peaches, green onion, lime juice, and honey in a small bowl.

2. Cover and chill at least 30 minutes. Serve with tortilla chips.

Nutrition Facts per Serving:

63 Calories; 0.5 g Total Fat (7% calories from fat); 0.1 g Saturated Fat; 12.9 g Carbohydrates; 2.4 g Protein; 0 mg Cholesterol; 2.0 g Fiber; 301 mg Sodium

Salsa—More Than a Dip

Salsa makes a great snack with tortilla chips, but there are so many more ways to use it as a simple, low-fat seasoning. Drizzle it over cooked chicken or pork; stir it into nonfat sour cream as a dipping sauce for chicken fingers; add it to cooked squash, beans, or potatoes; stir it into soups or rice; spread it over pot roast before cooking; or use it to marinate chicken, turkey, or pork.

CARROT TOPS

Dried onion soup mix makes a tasty seasoning to stir into cottage cheese for this calcium-packed snack. In addition to carrots, use squash slices or celery sticks for dipping.

Makes: 2 servings   Cost per Recipe: $0.82 Cost per Serving: $0.41

½ cup low-fat cottage cheese

1 teaspoon dried onion soup mix

20 carrot sticks

Nutrition Facts per Serving:

79 Calories; 0.7 g Total Fat (8% calories from fat); 0.4 g Saturated Fat; 10.5 g Carbohydrates; 7.7 g Protein; 2 mg Cholesterol; 1.9 g Fiber; 409 mg Sodium

1. Combine cottage cheese and dried onion soup mix in a small bowl. Divide mixture onto two small plates.

2. Arrange carrot sticks around cottage cheese mounds like a sunburst.

TIP What Are Baby Carrots?

"Baby" carrots look like tiny carrots, but actually they are cut from larger carrots. That extra process translates into extra cost, so cut your own carrot sticks from larger carrots to save money.

Eat Right for Less

DILLY DIP

This refreshing dip also can be served as a dressing over a summer salad of chopped cucumber, grapes, and fresh honeydew melon or used as a topping for salmon or fish fillets.

Makes: 2 servings   Cost per recipe: $0.65 Cost per serving: $0.33

½ cup fat-free plain yogurt

1½ teaspoons sugar

½ teaspoon lemon juice

½ teaspoon dried dillweed or 1½ teaspoons chopped fresh dillweed

½ small cucumber, sliced

1. Combine yogurt, sugar, lemon juice, and dill in a small bowl.

2. Serve with cucumber slices, other fresh vegetables, or pretzels.

Nutrition Facts per Serving:

43 Calories; 0.1 g Total Fat (2% calories from fat); 0 g Saturated Fat; 9.0 g Carbohydrates; 2.8 g Protein; 1 mg Cholesterol; 0.3 g Fiber; 35 mg Sodium

TIP Picking Cucumbers
Look for small to medium-sized cucumbers. Large ones tend to have lots of seeds and not as much flavor.

4-WAY POPCORN

Popcorn is a family favorite snack that's high in fiber. And, one or two simple ingredients kick ordinary popcorn up a notch! Pick your favorite flavor additions below. Just remember to check the label on the popcorn packages when you're shopping: the fat, calories, and sodium vary greatly among brands and varieties.

1 (3-ounce) bag low-fat, microwave popcorn or 4 cups freshly popped popcorn

Selected flavor variation

1. Pop the popcorn in a microwave oven according to package directions and transfer to a large bowl.

2. Add seasonings for one of the following variations to popcorn, mixing well.

ITALIAN-STYLE POPCORN

Makes: 3 servings
Cost per Recipe: $1.29
Cost per Serving: $0.43

1 tablespoon plus 2 teaspoons grated Parmesan cheese
1½ tablespoons garlic powder

Nutrition Facts per Serving:
146 Calories; 5.3 g Total Fat (31% calories from fat); 2.0 g Saturated Fat; 21.2 g Carbohydrates; 3.8 g Protein; 2 mg Cholesterol; 4.4 g Fiber; 334 mg Sodium

SPICY SWEET POPCORN

Makes: 3 servings
Cost per Recipe: $1.53
Cost per Serving: $0.51

1½ tablespoons ground cinnamon
1½ tablespoons light brown sugar

Nutrition Facts per Serving:
110 Calories; 3.5 g Total Fat (29% calories from fat); 1.1 g Saturated Fat; 19 g Carbohydrates; 1.6 g Protein; 0 mg Cholesterol; 4.4 g Fiber; 220 mg Sodium

PEPPERY POPCORN

Makes: 3 servings
Cost per Recipe: $0.96
Cost per Serving $0.32

1½ tablespoons black pepper

Nutrition Facts per Serving:
128 Calories; 4.6 g Total Fat (32% calories from fat); 1.5 g Saturated Fat; 20.1 g Carbohydrates; 2.4 g Protein; 0 mg Cholesterol; 4.4 g Fiber; 292 mg Sodium

RANCH-STYLE POPCORN

Makes: 3 servings
Cost per Recipe: $1.14
Cost per Serving: $0.38

1 tablespoon plus 2 teaspoons ranch dressing

Nutrition Facts per Serving:
120 Calories; 4.5 g Total Fat (34% calories from fat); 1.5 g Saturated Fat; 22.7 g Carbohydrates; 2.0 g Protein; 0 mg Cholesterol; 4.4 g Fiber; 944 mg Sodium

Eat Right for Less

SNACKIN' MIX

This mix makes 9½ cups—plenty for a party, or for keeping around for a healthy whole grain snack. If you aren't having a party, package ½-cup servings in individual zip-top plastic bags and store them in the freezer. This trick helps keep the snack mix fresh, and helps you with portion control.

Makes: 19 (½-cup) servings   Cost per Recipe: $3.72   Cost per Serving: $0.20

3 tablespoons butter

½ teaspoon garlic powder

½ teaspoon onion salt

2 teaspoons lemon juice

1½ tablespoons Worcestershire sauce

7 cups toasted whole wheat cereal squares

½ cup mixed honey roasted peanuts or mixed nuts

2 cups pretzel twists or sticks

Nutrition Facts per Serving:

84 Calories; 3.3 g Total Fat (35% calories from fat); 1.3 g Saturated Fat; 12.7 g Carbohydrates; 2.1 g Protein; 5 mg Cholesterol; 1.5 g Fiber; 227 mg Sodium

1. Place butter in a microwave-safe measuring cup or bowl. Microwave on HIGH 20 seconds or until melted. Stir in garlic powder, onion salt, lemon juice, and Worcestershire sauce.

2. Combine cereal, nuts, and pretzels in a large microwave-safe bowl. Pour butter mixture over cereal mixture and mix well. Microwave on HIGH 2 minutes. Stir, and microwave on HIGH 2 more minutes.

3. Spread snack mix in single layer on paper towels or waxed paper to cool. Mixture will become crisp after cooling.

TIP How to Avoid Temptation

Vending machines and fast food restaurants can be a great temptation when you're hungry. You can avoid the extra expense of these "quick-fix," high-calorie foods by planning ahead. Keep carrot sticks, celery sticks, or grapes washed and ready for grabbing from the fridge. Package a small bag of whole grain cereal snack mix or popcorn for your car. Or, instead of reaching for a snack, first chew a stick of sugar-free gum, which can help curb the munchies.

FRUITY YOGURT POPS

If you have popsicle sticks on hand, you can poke them into the yogurt through the foil on top of the cup before freezing the pops. Then, just tear away the cup beginning at the top as you eat the frozen snack.

Makes: 6 servings   Cost per Recipe: $1.44   Cost per Serving: $0.24

2 cups chopped fresh or frozen fruit (blueberries, raspberries, strawberries, bananas)

2 cups fat-free plain yogurt

¼ cup sugar

Nutrition Facts per Yogurt Pop:

93 Calories; 0.2 g Total Fat (2% calories from fat); 0.0 g Saturated Fat; 21.6 g Carbohydrates; 3.8 g Protein; 2 mg Cholesterol; 1.6 g Fiber; 46 mg Sodium

1. Combine fruit, yogurt, and sugar in a bowl, mixing well. (Or, combine ingredients in a blender and process until smooth.)

2. Pour mixture into popsicle molds or six 5-ounce paper cups. Cover with aluminum foil. Freeze at least 5 hours. To remove pop from cup, place bottom of cup under warm, running water 15 seconds.

TIP Fast, Fun Snack Idea
Place seedless grapes in a freezer-proof container and freeze. When you're hungry for a cool snack, take a few straight from the freezer, pop in your mouth, and enjoy!

Eat Right for Less

FAMILY MENUS

HOT AND HEARTY OATMEAL BREAKFAST

SERVES 6

Banana Bread Oatmeal (page 16)
Whole Wheat Toast
Peanut Butter and Blueberry Jam
Orange Juice
Fat-Free Milk

This is a great menu for family, but it will impress company, too. Just make sure you have bananas on hand. Here's an idea to be ready to make this recipe anytime.

When you have extra-ripe bananas, peel and mash them. Place the mashed banana into cups in a muffin pan and put the pan in the freezer until the bananas are frozen. Pop out the frozen banana cups and store them together in a plastic zip-top freezer bag.

The banana may darken but it won't matter in this recipe because you'll be stirring it into oatmeal. You can add a teaspoon of lemon juice for each mashed banana to prevent it from turning brown, if you wish.

NO-TIME-TO-EAT BREAKFAST

SERVES 3

Ham & Cheese Muffins (page 10)
Pineapple Banana Smoothie (page 17)

Breakfast is the most important meal of the day. If you have family members who rush out each morning without taking time to eat, here's a menu you can put in their hands as they leave. Make the Ham and Cheese Muffins ahead of time and store them in the freezer in a plastic zip-top freezer bag. Pop the number you need in the microwave for just a few seconds and they'll be ready to eat on the run.

If you don't have a blender to make the smoothie, just put apple slices in a zip-top plastic bag and fat-free milk in a to-go cup and you've fed your on-the-go family a healthy meal.

Eat Right for Less

SNOWY DAY SOUP & SANDWICH LUNCH

SERVES 4

Heartfelt Tuna Melts (page 37)
Hot Tomato Soup
Honeyed Carrot Salad (page 44)

Snowed in? The best thing about this hearty lunch menu is that if you have the basic food staples in your pantry and refrigerator, you have everything you need on hand for a hearty lunch or light supper. Make the tomato soup with milk for even more nutrition. And, you can make the carrot salad to serve right away, or prepare it in advance and serve it cold from the fridge.

But don't wait for a snowy day to enjoy this menu combination. Tuna is healthy for your heart. An ideal diet includes fish at least two times a week.

FAMILY FAVORITE CHICKEN DINNER

SERVES 8

Easy Mozzarella Chicken Bake (page 21)
Hot Cooked Rice or Spaghetti
Green Beans
Toasted French Bread Slices
Applesauce

If you assemble the chicken casserole the night before and store it in the refrigerator before baking, you can have this meal on the table in less than 30 minutes. While the casserole bakes, cook the rice or pasta, steam the green beans, and slice and toast the bread. Keep a can of applesauce in the refrigerator—it'll taste better chilled. To make applesauce an extra special dessert treat, sprinkle each serving with a dash of ground cinnamon.

SUMMERTIME SANDWICH SUPPER

SERVES 6

Herbed Turkey Burgers (page 23)
Layered Mexican Salad (page 40)
Watermelon Wedges

Whether you cook them in a skillet or on an outdoor grill, burgers make any meal a treat. Use fresh herbs (in season during spring and summer) if you have them; the burgers will taste even better. Mexican Salad requires no cooking—a perfect choice for hot summer days—so make it ahead of time and pull it from the refrigerator when you're ready to serve.

For dessert, look for good buys on peaches, watermelon, berries, plums, and cantaloupe in the peak of flavor for this menu. Any fresh fruit is good with these flavorful burgers, so serve your family's favorite in place of watermelon for a sweet, healthy end to the meal.

SPECIAL OCCASION PORK CHOP DINNER

SERVES 8

Marinated Pineapple Pork Chops (page 30)
Baked Sweet Potatoes
Steamed Broccoli
Whole Wheat Rolls
Chocolate Cherry Trifle (page 54)

Who says you have to sweat in the kitchen making a meal to celebrate a birthday, an accomplishment, or a special occasion? Just a little planning will help you put this meal on the table with little effort. The night before, make the dessert trifle and put the pork chops in the refrigerator to marinate. Bake the sweet potatoes in the microwave while you steam the broccoli. The pork chops broil in about 10 minutes.

Serve the sweet potatoes with brown sugar and cinnamon, and the broccoli with lemon juice or grated Parmesan cheese for low-fat seasoning options.

Eat Right for Less

HOT AND FILLING CAJUN-STYLE DINNER

SERVES 6

Cajun Beef & Bean Stew (page 26)
Hot Cooked Rice
Fruited Coleslaw (page 43)
Orange-Spiced Bananas with Ice Cream (page 56)

This menu will give you a flavor of New Orleans and time to spare! Let the stew cook all day in a slow cooker and you're ready to serve right from the pot at dinnertime. Make the coleslaw ahead of time to serve crunchy and cold with the hot and tender beef stew. It takes less than 10 minutes to whip up the warm banana sauce to serve over fat-free ice cream.

If you don't have a slow cooker, cook the stew on top of the stove for 2 to 3 hours, then refrigerate it. The flavor is actually better the next day as the flavors blend. Just heat it up when you're ready to serve.

LASAGNA NIGHT

SERVES 8

Vegetable Lasagna (page 32)
Spinach Salad with Chopped Apple
Fat-Free Balsamic Dressing
Sliced Whole Wheat Italian Loaf
Layered Peanut Butter-Chocolate Parfaits (page 53)

Who doesn't love lasagna? And, lasagna night at your house can be easy... prepare this lasagna up to the point of baking, and refrigerate it (to bake in the next 2 days) or freeze it to have a meal ready to thaw and bake. The lasagna is the only part of the meal you cook. While it bakes, you can assemble the salad and no-cook dessert.

ONE-POT ROAST BEEF DINNER

SERVES 12

Juicy Pot Roast with Vegetables (page 27)
Cornbread Muffins
Apple Wedges
Fat-Free Chocolate Ice Cream

Whether you use a slow cooker or simmer this pot roast on top of the stove, it's a one-dish meal that makes dinner easy for the cook. The roast simmers with potatoes and carrots, so all you have to do is add some warm corn muffins and the meal's complete. This recipe uses rump roast, but other less expensive and less tender beef cuts can be substituted. The long, slow cooking process makes the meat juicy and fork-tender.

DINNER FROM THE GARDEN

SERVES UP TO 12

Garden Pasta Salad (page 49)
Low-Fat Cottage Cheese with
Fresh Cucumber and Tomato
Corn on the Cob
Cantaloupe Wedges

There's nothing more delicious than a tableful of fruits and vegetables straight from the garden or the farmers' market when everything tastes sweetest. If you don't have a farmers' market, look for local produce in your supermarket; many stores are making an effort to buy from nearby farmers.

During the hot months, this pasta salad makes use of the fresh produce. You can serve it warm or chilled from the refrigerator. So, if you have some left over, it's ready to serve with another meal anytime.

Eat Right for Less

BASIC STAPLES

Dashing to the store at the last minute is the pits. What a waste of prime time! Keep these basic staples stashed in the pantry ... and cooking's cool.

FREEZER

- Bread
- Fish
- Frozen vegetables
- Lean ground beef
- Orange juice
- Whole chicken or pieces

REFRIGERATOR

- Carrots
- Cheese – shredded, sliced
- Eggs
- Grated Parmesan cheese
- Low-fat salad dressing
- Margarine/Butter
- Milk
- Plain yogurt

CANNED AND DRY GOODS

- Beans – canned or dried
- Crackers
- Crunchy cereal
- Macaroni/Pasta
- Miscellaneous fruits & vegetables
- Mushrooms
- Oats
- Peanut butter
- Pizza/Pasta sauce
- Rice
- Tomatoes – diced, whole, juice, sauce, stewed
- Tuna
- Vegetable broth

PANTRY STAPLE SEASONING ITEMS

- Basil
- Bay leaves
- Black pepper
- Bouillon
- Chili powder
- Cinnamon
- Cream of tartar
- Dill
- Garlic powder
- Ginger
- Italian seasoning
- Lemon Juice
- Onion flakes
- Oregano
- Paprika
- Rosemary
- Salt
- Soy sauce
- Thyme
- Vanilla
- Vinegar
- Worcestershire sauce

PANTRY STAPLE BAKING ITEMS

- Baking powder
- Baking soda
- Canola or olive oil
- Cornstarch
- Dried fruit (raisins)
- Dry milk
- Flour
- Sliced almonds (or other nuts)
- Sugar – powdered, white, brown

SEASONAL GUIDE TO FRESH FRUITS & VEGETABLES

SUMMER

Beets
Bell peppers
Blackberries
Blueberries
Broccoli
Chinese cabbage
Chile peppers
Corn
Cucumbers
Eggplant
Green beans
Nectarines
Okra
Peaches
Plums
Raspberries
Summer squash
Tomatoes
Watermelon
Zucchini

FALL

Acorn squash
Apples
Butternut squash
Cauliflower
Figs
Garlic
Grapes
Leaf lettuce
Mushrooms
Parsnips
Pears
Pomegranate
Pumpkin
Sweet potatoes

WINTER

Brussels sprouts
Grapefruit
Kale
Leeks
Lemons
Oranges
Radishes
Tangerines
Turnips

SPRING

Apricots
Asparagus
Avocado
Cabbage
Carrots
Collards
Mango
Mustard greens
New potatoes
Pineapple
Rhubarb
Spinach
Spring baby lettuce
Strawberries
Sugar snap and snow peas
Vidalia onions

Eat Right for Less

TOP 20 HEALTHY RECIPE SUBSTITUTIONS

	Original Ingredient	Healthy Substitute (equal amount)
1	1 Large whole egg (¼ cup)—*WARNING: When baking, substitute egg whites for half of the whole eggs, or the product may be tough.*	2 Large egg whites, ¼ cup egg whites or egg substitute
2	2% or whole milk	Skim, ½% or 1% milk
3	Heavy cream	Soups/casseroles—evaporated skim milk Baking—light cream or half & half
4	Coffee cream or half & half	Whole milk or evaporated skim milk
5	Buttermilk	2% buttermilk or 15 Tbsp skim milk + 1 Tbsp lemon juice
6	Evaporated whole milk	Evaporated skim milk
7	Sweetened condensed whole milk	Low-fat or nonfat sweetened condensed milk
8	Sour cream & yogurt—*WARNING: If recipe requires cooking, use nonfat only in sweet recipes.*	Low-fat or nonfat
9	Cream cheese—*WARNING: Nonfat produces dips and cake frosting that are very runny.*	Light cream cheese
10	Cottage cheese & ricotta cheese	Low-fat or dry curds
11	Butter—*WARNING: Light/low-fat margarines contain more water and may cause a baked product to be tough, so try decreasing regular margarine 1 to 2 Tbsp first.*	Margarine
12	Regular cheese (block or shredded)—*WARNING: Do not use nonfat in cooked foods, because it does not melt.*	Low-fat or nonfat
13	1 cup cheddar cheese 1 cup grated Parmesan cheese	¾ cup very sharp or sharp cheddar cheese ¾ cup fresh shredded Parmesan cheese
14	1 oz. unsweetened baking chocolate	3 Tbsp dry cocoa + 2 tsp sugar + 1 Tbsp oil
15	1 cup chocolate chips	½ cup mini chocolate chips
16	1 cup oil in quick breads (muffins, breads)	½ cup baby fruit or vegetable + ½ cup oil or 1% buttermilk
17	Regular peanut butter	Reduced fat peanut butter
18	1 cup chopped pecans or walnuts	½ cup nuts toasted to bring out the flavor
19	1 cup shredded coconut	½ cup toasted coconut + ½ tsp coconut extract
20	Mayonnaise & salad dressing—*WARNING: Do not cook with nonfat versions, because they turn sweet with heat.*	Light or nonfat

List compiled by Cheryl H. Armstrong, MBA, RD, CD, for the Nutrition and Food Safety Workshop for Quantity Food /Providers, April 27, 1999.

ACKNOWLEDGMENTS

The Purdue University Family Nutrition Program expresses appreciation to the following organizations, companies, and cookbook authors who generously shared their recipes or inspired other recipes in this cookbook. For more recipes and food information from these sources, you'll find their contact information below.

Alaska Seafood

Website: www.alaskaseafood.org
Email: info@alaskaseafood.org
Phone: 1-800-806-2497
Address: 150 Nickerson Street, Suite 310
          Seattle, WA 98109-1634

American Egg Board

Website: www.IncredibleEgg.org
Email: aeb@aeb.org
Phone: 847-296-7043
Address: 1460 Renaissance Drive
          Park Ridge, IL 60068

Cabot Creamery

Website: www.cabotcheese.coop
Phone: 1-888-792-2268
Address: 1 Home Farm Way
          Montpelier, VT 05602

California Cling Peach Board

Website: www.calclingpeach.com
Email: capeach@echopr.com
Phone: 559-595-1425
Address: 1195 Park Avenue, Suite 212
          Emeryville, CA 94608

Eggland's Best

Website: www.egglandsbest.com
Phone: 800-922-EGGS (3447)
Address: 1400 South Trooper Road
          Suite 201, Jeffersonville, PA 19403

Holly Clegg

Author of *Holly Clegg's trim&TERRIFIC Gulf Coast Favorites*
Website: www.hollyclegg.com

Nancy Slagle and Carol Santee

Authors of *30-Day Gourmet's Big Book of Freezer Cooking*
Website: www.30daygourmet.com
Address: 30 Day Gourmet, Inc., P.O. Box 272
          Brownsburg, IN 46112

National Pork Board

Website: www.TheOtherWhiteMeat.com
Email: info@pork.org
Phone: 1-515-223-2600

Quaker Oats Company

Website: www.quakeroats.com
Phone: 1-800-FOR-OATS (367-6287)
Address: P.O. Box 049003
          Chicago, IL 60604-9003

Elizabeth M. Ward, M.S., R.D.

Author of *Expect the Best, Your Guide to Healthy Eating Before, During, & After Pregnancy*
Website: www.expectthebestpregnancy.com

Eat Right for Less

RECIPE INDEX

Eat Right for Less

ABOUT US

The mission of **Purdue University Nutrition Education Programs** *(NEP) is to empower limited resource audiences to: make healthy food choices, prepare safe meals, use food dollars wisely and engage in regular physical activity to enhance the quality of life.*

Two Nutrition Education Programs that strive to serve low-income Hoosiers will be present in 90 of Indiana's 92 counties in 2011:

▶ The Family Nutrition Program (FNP)

▶ The Expanded Food and Nutrition Education Program (EFNEP)

For more information on nutrition, food budgeting,
and food safety, visit

www.www.enjoyfoodbeactive.org

The mission of the **Purdue Cooperative Extension Service** *is the education of the Indiana citizens through application of the land-grant university research and knowledge base for the benefit of agriculture, youth, families, and communities.*

www.ag.purdue.edu/extension

For information on similiar products from Purdue Extension,
visit The Education Store online

www.the-education-store.com